42 Rules for 24-Hour Success on LinkedIn

By Chris Muccio
with Peggy Murrah

E-mail: info@superstarpress.com
20660 Stevens Creek Blvd., Suite 210
Cupertino, CA 95014

Published by Super Star Press™, a THiNKaha® imprint
20660 Stevens Creek Blvd., Suite 210, Cupertino, CA 95014
http://42rules.com

2nd Edition: August 2013
1st Edition: May 2009
Paperback ISBN (2nd Edition): 978-1-60773-100-9 (1-60773-100-2)
Paperback ISBN (1st Edition): 978-1-60773-018-7 (1-60773-018-9)

eBook ISBN: 978-1-60773-019-4 (1-60773-019-7)
Place of Publication: Silicon Valley, California, USA
Library of Congress Number: 2008940965

Trademarks

All terms mentioned in this book that are known to be trademarks or service marks have been appropriately capitalized. THiNKaha® nor any of its imprints, can attest to the accuracy of this information. Use of a term in this book should not be regarded as affecting the validity of any trademark or service mark.

Warning and Disclaimer

Every effort has been made to make this book as complete and as accurate as possible. The information provided is on an "as is" basis. The author(s), publisher, and its agents assume no responsibility for errors or omissions nor assume liability or responsibility to any person or entity with respect to any loss or damages arising from the use of information contained herein.

Praise for This Book

"One of the lessons I have learned in marketing and selling (without be- ing "sales-y") is the importance of providing value and being authentic. Social media is an important tool for connecting with people. LinkedIn particularly is a way to share value and generate leads.

"Colleagues have shared with me they don't see how LinkedIn can be a powerful lead generation tool for entrepreneurs. When I hear this, I think of Chris Muccio and Peggy Murrah and their book, 42 Rules for 24-Hour Success on LinkedIn. They share a unique way to strategize, attract, engage, and convert leads on LinkedIn. This is easily one of my top business reads for learning how LinkedIn can transform your busi- ness by growing your list, connecting with more high value customers, and increasing your sales."
Lisa Sasevich, The Queen of Sales Conversion

"LinkedIn has quickly emerged as a powerful networking tool, and 42 Rules for 24-Hour Success on LinkedIn *is a terrific actionable guide to help the savvy professional leverage LinkedIn effectively. The rules provide a strategic framework that enables the user to quickly build their LinkedIn network and, more importantly, use that network to drive their LinkedIn 'brand' to deliver results, opportunities, and action."*
Alex Sevilla, Assistant Dean & Director of MBA Programs, The University of Florida

*"*42 Rules for 24-Hour Success on LinkedIn *provides straightforward, common-sense advice on how to get the most out of LinkedIn, the most popular social networking site for busy professionals. In this compact book, Chris and Peggy show you what to do to leverage the power of social networking on LinkedIn. And they do it in an easy- to-use, enjoyable read. If you want to build a network of like-minded professionals, you need to be on LinkedIn. If you're on LinkedIn, you need to read* 42 Rules for 24-Hour Success on LinkedIn.*"*
Bud Bilanich, The Common Sense Guy, Bestselling Author of *Straight Talk for Success*

"LinkedIn is the critical social media for business professionals. This book gives you the strategies and tactics to build your LinkedIn profile and to generate real business opportunities. Chris and Peggy give you concise and action-oriented approaches to succeed with LinkedIn."
Jay Berkowitz, Author, *The Ten Golden Rules of Online Marketing Workbook* (www.TenGoldenRules.com)

"Amazing! In this timely and cutting-edge book, the authors share their secrets to increasing your ROI on your online networking efforts. They give an abundance of tips and strategies to develop relationships using LinkedIn. Learn how to automate and leverage relationships through social fusion. I strongly recommend this book to anyone that wants to increase their sales results. If you want to build visibility and develop profitable relationships, read this book!"
Rick S. Cooper, MBA, The Sales Results Expert,
http://rickscooper.com

"From a business perspective, social networking is changing every day with new technology, tools, and strategies. With so many options at our fingertips, users are challenged simply by trying to determine where to begin and how to effectively use these tools. Given this bewildering landscape, the book 42 Rules for 24-Hour Success on LinkedIn *ties it all together quite simply and provides excellent practical tips and advice on how to effectively embrace this change."*
J. John Simione, Senior Vice President, MARSH,
http://marsh.com

"Reading this book will give you a solid foundation for your LinkedIn strategy!"
Jason Alba, CEO, JibberJobber.com, Author, *I'm on LinkedIn—Now What???*

"The digital insight in this book is very powerful! Strategies, tactics, and success stories. This book has it all and presents it simply, logically, and in a very actionable manner. This is a highly recommended read."
Enrique Porras, Chief Digital Officer

"These 42 rules provide entrepreneurs, corporations, and job seekers with gems of advice and are the perfect resource to make sense of how they can generate success with LinkedIn. For new users, it provides a terrific overview; for experienced users, it is a great reminder of the things they may know intuitively but may have forgotten in the rush of their hectic schedules."
Michael Port, Author, *Book Yourself Solid, The Contrarian Effect*

Acknowledgments

Writing and marketing a book may seem like a very cool thing (and some of it truly is), but it is a very time-consuming task. It ultimately encompassed every element of my life and required the support of many special people. Without these people, I would not have been able to achieve what was accomplished in such a short period of time.

There are a lot of people I want to acknowledge and offer my heartfelt thanks to. I couldn't start this list off without thanking my wife, Aneesa. She has been my perpetual supporter from day one, be it patiently waiting for me to finish writing "just one more phrase" or getting up with me at 5:30 a.m. just so she could be in the front row of an event I was speaking at.

My mother comes next, and not because of her technical acumen. Actually, when I first described the use of the "cloud" to her, she looked up at the sky and said, "Really? Up there?" While she may not understand what I'm talking about or how it functions, she has never once stopped encouraging me to pursue something I believe in.

In 2007, I met my coauthor, Peggy Murrah. Since then we have worked together on a number of cutting-edge digital marketing ideas. Peggy's roles typically end up with her behind the scenes, but I want to make sure to bring her front and center and let her know how thankful I am for all of her contributions.

In May 2013, I met Jessica Wald, a business student at the State University of New York at Albany. Her help on the marketing of this book was spot on. She has been one of the best young people I've had the privilege of working with. This young lady has a very bright future in front of her.

The topic of this book is focused on success stories. How could this have been written without great people who were willing to take the time to talk and share their stories with us? While their names are mentioned in this book, I want to specifically thank each and every one of them here too! A big heartfelt thanks to Susan Harrow, Bruce Rector, Gaida Zirkelbach, Des Walsh, Jay Deragon, Vince Gelormine, Lorraine Ball, Cindy Kraft, Antoine Dupont, Chad Van Horn, Susan Kaplan, Michael Daszkal, Kris Gilbertson, and Mary Agnes Antonopoulos.

I would also like to thank David Burns, who was a key contributor to the first edition, for the many conversations we've had over the years that have inspired me.

Without all of you, there would be no second edition. Thank you! Thank you!! Thank you!!! You are the best!

Chris

Contents

Interest. That singular word is what drives digital business development—no, not interest from the financial standpoint, but interest from the perspective of those seeking information.

What tools are at our disposal for seeking information? Ask a friend, seek a referral, or perhaps go online and seek an answer from Google.

How often do you use Google to search for something? Actually, there are over one billion searches per day all over the world. This common feature of seeking information directly leads to a multibillion-dollar process.

While there may be over a billion searches per day and Google may be one of the world's largest companies, this is not a story about search engine optimization; this is a story about an integrated approach to digital marketing, specifically through LinkedIn. Interestingly, many businesses miss out on using LinkedIn to generate new business leads, even though it should be an integral part of their sales and marketing process.

When we wrote the first edition of this book, we shared a story about going fishing and explained LinkedIn in terms of baiting your hook and waiting to catch a fish. In this edition, we would like to draw upon another analogy and compare generating results from marketing to improving your golf game.

Let's say you decide one day that you want to play golf like a pro. What do you need to do? You'll need to assess the skill level of your existing short game, long game, mental game, and putting game. In addition, you'll need to know how much time and money you have to focus every day on improving these four areas.

There are also dependencies that will impact your ability to generate "results" in golf. Are you learning from a video or from a professional instructor? How much time does your instructor have to work with you? How good are the others that you will be playing against? Are you able to work on each element of your game in line with the others or does one have to be perfected before the other?

Can you play like a pro in less than three months? It's possible, but unless you come with all the prerequisite skills, it's not likely.

The requirements for generating results in golf are similar to digital business development. There are multiple elements that need to be maximized and integrated together. On top of that, the impact on each person or business is going to be different based on their unique circumstances.

In this book, we are going to focus on generating leads across LinkedIn. While this book is technically a second edition, for all intents and purposes, it is a new book. We will dig into strategies and their supporting tactics. Something new we've done this time is interview people that have generated success, and we've added their stories so you can learn from them.

Our guess is that you are very interested in learning what is required to generate more leads and more revenue, which is why you purchased this book. We can't guarantee you specific results, but we think it is fair to suggest specific action paths and forecast what they might ultimately drive. Those that dig into this book and apply it as thoroughly as is required will see results. Depending on your industry type and the path required, some of you will get fantastic results, while others will have more modest ones. That is simply the fact of the way the world works. Anyone telling you differently is glossing over the truth.

Throughout this book, we provide you with free tools to enhance the insights you will learn. Just type in the links provided, and enjoy their benefits. Now it's time to kick off your roadmap for results. We wish you much success on your path!

Section I
The Basics

Why are you on LinkedIn? Do you understand how you can most effectively benefit from it?

While signing on and using LinkedIn may be straightforward, generating results from your usage of LinkedIn requires sophistication. These rules introduce you to this "sophistication," which we describe in terms of a four-part methodology:

(1) Strategize

(2) Attract

(3) Engage

(4) Convert

Rule 1: Rules Are Meant to Be Broken

Rule 2: Answer the Most Important Questions First

Rule 3: Get LinkedIn or Get Left Out?

Rule 4: I've Been on LinkedIn and It Doesn't Work

Rule 5: Overcome the Overwhelm

Rule 6: Consider the ROI

Rule 7: What Does a LinkedIn Lead Look Like?

1 Rules Are Meant to Be Broken

What makes us different makes LinkedIn great!

Who is the typical LinkedIn user? LinkedIn claims a membership that is growing at a rate of more than two people per second,[1] yet there really is not a typical "user." If you look around, you will find people who work solo and use LinkedIn as the proverbial office water cooler—a place to go to interact, share stories, and be part of a community. This type of user might be using LinkedIn for personal and social development.

Then there are the people who create their own income. This can range from the one-person independent consultant to the managing partner of a consulting practice, from the small-business owner to the commissioned sales professional. It includes everyone who generates his or her own income streams. Yes, they encounter a significant amount of risk, but they also tend to lean toward an entrepreneurial way of thinking as they prospect for new, efficient, and effective ways to generate revenue streams. Their interest generally lies in business development.

Shifting the risk profile, you also shift the perspective of the user to those who prefer the stability of a steady income. This can include anyone from the job seeker to the professional looking to manage a career path. While these people may have entrepreneurial inclinations,

---

[1] "About LinkedIn," *LinkedIn,* accessed August 2013, http://press.linkedin.com/about/.

their income stream is not dependent on generating new sales. Instead, it is dependent on their ability to manage, lead, work in groups, build relationships, and generally help their employer in an effective manner. Any dollar they add to the business, they generally don't see. While they may understand that communication on LinkedIn can drive additional revenue, it is not their priority for participating on LinkedIn. Their priority is to stay plugged into a professional network that can help them leverage their career development.

When this book was initially published, companies had minimal presences on LinkedIn. Today, over 2.8 million have a company profile on the site.

What makes us different makes LinkedIn great! The one commonality is that all these users are looking for some sort of development and benefit from LinkedIn, yet, clearly, benefiting from LinkedIn means something different to almost every person.

As you read through this book, our rules take an approach that does not try to be everything to everyone. Instead, we follow a natural strategic development process where concepts build upon themselves. Not all the rules are going to apply to each type of user, and, even for those that do, there may be a variety of ways to achieve similar results. So while we don't advocate going against the netiquette and norms established throughout social media, we do expect that you will use the rules as a flexible guide and bend or even break them if you see more effective ways to achieve a particular goal.

To further increase the effectiveness of this book for you, we have created a free downloadable workbook. Simply go to www.LeadGen2020.com/workbook, sign up, and download it for free. This workbook is a stand-alone resource as well as a companion for these 42 rules. You will find a wide range of tips, questions, comments, etc. that will help you support your 24-hour success!

2 Answer the Most Important Questions First

LinkedIn is a communication tool. It is a place to find people and be found.

Let's start with a question: *Why are you on LinkedIn?*

On the surface, this seems to be a simple question: only five words and none were more than 10 letters long. But it seems that whenever we ask that question, we're asking something on par with an existential question like, "What is the meaning of life?" because the response we get nine times out of 10 is a contemplative silence. So we try to break the uneasy silence by asking another question, "What was your encouragement to register on LinkedIn?" and with that, a big smile usually appears and people say, "Oh, I received an invitation to sign up." To which our reply is, "That's great, what are your goals for being registered on LinkedIn?" This time, the responses range from that contemplative silence to the ambitious "Gain more clients."

LinkedIn is a place for business professionals to be "found" and "to find" people. It is a vehicle to communicate. It is a tool to use with your business, in your career management, your education, your social endeavors, and probably a whole lot more. Yes, you can turn contacts into clients, and yes, you can turn prospects into customers, but by itself, LinkedIn is not a magic elixir.

So, as we begin this book, we pose some questions for you to think about:

- Why are you on LinkedIn? Do you understand how you can most effectively benefit from it?

- What are you looking to achieve with LinkedIn? Are your goals realistic? Have you created a strategy and supported it with realistic action items?

- How are you showing initiative? You are reading these rules, so that indicates you have the drive and commitment to learn. What else are you doing to enhance your ability to achieve the goals you've established on LinkedIn? For instance, if you are on it to network, are you networking? What have you been doing to build relationships?

- How much time are you fitting into your schedule to properly participate and execute on your strategy? Unfortunately, this is not the field of dreams (i.e., build it and they will come). Without allocating time in your busy schedule to work on your action plan, you may end up more like a billboard in a jungle—bright and shiny but not seen by many people.

To reiterate, success on LinkedIn is not like rubbing the magic lantern and having the genie immediately appear. 24-hour success should not imply immediate gratification. What 24-hour success implies is literally setting yourself up for success by doing all the "right" things that will eventually help you succeed. In the wired world we live in, success can occur during the middle of the business day, when you are sitting in front of your computer, or while you are sleeping in bed.

3 Get LinkedIn or Get Left Out?

The old cliché is that success is not based on what you know but rather who you know. Understanding your online identity is critical to creating success, and LinkedIn is currently one of the most powerful tools that can help you.

LinkedIn is a communication platform. In business, we use a variety of platforms from e-commerce to customer relationship management tools to accounting tools and more. However, we typically don't blindly jump into any of them and expect to have any sort of success. Conversely, what we do is start with a strategy and then build out our platforms so that they become effective tools for our business.

While signing on and using LinkedIn may be straightforward, generating results from your usage of LinkedIn requires sophistication. We summarize this sophistication with a four-part methodology you will see throughout this book:

Download it for free at www.LeadGen2020.com/methodology.

(1) Strategize

(2) Attract

(3) Engage

(4) Convert

But... I Don't Have a Lot of Free Time to Do This

As successful professionals, your time is valuable, and what you choose to focus on must provide you with an effective result. Perhaps you might be thinking the following right about now: "This sounds great, but there are only 24 hours in a day and I have a business to run, so realistically speaking, how much time should I focus on using this tool?"

Basically, there is no hard and fast rule. The most truthful answer is, "It depends." What does it depend on? What type of business do you have? How do you generate your leads? What are you currently focusing on with your business? What are your current business needs? How much time have you already spent in building a responsive network? Of course, there are quite a few more questions to consider too.

Some companies will never generate meaningful leads quite simply because they don't know how to use this tool, while others can spend a few minutes per day and generate a nice flow of leads. Throughout this book, we will share success stories of what people have accomplished on LinkedIn and the paths they've pursued to achieve those accomplishments. If we were to suggest a baseline for time, we would suggest setting expectations of about 15 minutes per day (once you've gotten beyond the initial setup), but expect some days to require more as you get more engaged.

Caveats to Our Time Suggestion

First, you need to follow an effective and focused approach to using this tool, such as the four-part methodology we will be focusing on in this book. This is key to managing your time.

Secondly, and most importantly, you must **sustain** your effort. This sounds like the most basic concept, but it is very important to adhere to it. Unfortunately, many people join and collect contacts but invest no time or energy networking, so they gain nothing from the site. This is a clear example of reaping what you have sown. Remember, LinkedIn is just a tool to connect and open doors, but it still takes work on your part to make it effective.

If you would like to connect with us as you build out your program, please follow the links to our profiles:

http://LinkedIn.com/in/ChrisMuccio

http://LinkedIn.com/in/PeggyMurrah

Send us an invite **noting that you've read the book,** and we'd be very happy to accept your invitation.

4 I've Been on LinkedIn and It Doesn't Work

Social media will change your business; catch up or catch you later.

Five years ago, in the infancy of social media, *Businessweek* had a great headline: "Social Media Will Change Your Business"; the article advised readers to "catch up...or catch you later."[2] However, five years later, people are still struggling with how to "catch up." Let's begin to shed light on this in this rule. Too many people think that just by having a profile on LinkedIn, they'll get leads and new business.

In typical day-to-day, face-to-face networking, when people are asked about their usage of LinkedIn, it seems that most people share the same experience. They sign up for LinkedIn, gather some contacts, and search out people they may know from schools, prior employers, or from professional associations. Once they've tapped that out, they are lost as to what to do next or how to realize any benefits from being on LinkedIn.

With millions of users and growing daily, LinkedIn offers a variety of opportunities to quickly connect with a vast audience to enhance the potential for your career and business success, but why isn't everyone achieving immediate success?

---

[2] Stephen Baker and Heather Green, "Social Media Will Change Your Business," *Businessweek,* February 20, 2008, http://www.businessweek.com/stories/2008-02-20/social-media-will-change-your-businessbusinessweek-business-news-stock-market-and-financial-advice.

Understand the Type of "Business Race" You Are In

Question: Do you think you would prepare differently for a marathon versus a sprint? If you are looking to do very well, it would seem that you would prepare as appropriately as possible considering the preparation for each is uniquely different.

When you are using LinkedIn for lead generation, it is not a sprint. It is an ongoing series of interactions with your target audience. Generating results on LinkedIn starts with having a focus and a purpose when you begin. Then you focus on attracting people to you, and once those people are connected to you, you need to engage them. The most effective way to do this is quite simple: provide these people value that is relevant to them and their business. This takes time, and the process needs to be sustained. Throughout this book, we offer both strategy and tactics for you to use to achieve this as efficiently as possible.

Two Unspoken Perspectives of What LinkedIn Is and What It Is Not

Profile and Company Pages

- While these are relatively easy to create, they don't automatically generate leads or revenue because they aren't designed to. They are designed to "tell" who we are and what we do and hopefully let others see how great we think we are. However, when used effectively in an integrated strategy, they can be conduits for lead gen.

LinkedIn Compared to Facebook or Twitter

- LinkedIn may share similarities with Facebook and Twitter, but it is clearly not the same platform. While those sites have significant personal interaction through comments or pictures, LinkedIn lacks the personal and often meaningless information that clutters up Facebook and Twitter. Instead, LinkedIn is where people come to showcase their careers and find information relevant to their professional lives, making it an invaluable resource for businesses. In short, LinkedIn moves beyond simply being a tool to connect with former colleagues and college friends to being a great tool in your overall marketing and sales tool belt.

Here's How It Works Best

We read the following perspective, and wish we could remember where so we could give its author proper recognition, but to the person who wrote this phrase, you expressed the sentiment to this rule well:

Put something of value in your company page and profile and now you'll get readers.

Give them compelling reasons to visit your site and engage your company and now you'll get prospects.

Continue to communicate the value your prospects are seeking and then you can get SALES!

5 Overcome the Overwhelm

Many people are struggling to understand where to begin, and just as many are simply trying to find out how to properly participate.

In the five years since this book was originally written, a fairly common issue we've heard is that some LinkedIn users aren't exactly sure of the proper etiquette and are afraid of breaching it, so they barely participate, which of course minimizes their opportunity to generate results.

LinkedIn offers a whole new marketing capability with your prospects, your customers, your business partners, and your employees. Therefore, we need to remove the roadblocks to effectively pursue results. As such, this rule will add guidance to help you navigate through the "participation puzzle."

Create Effective Participation through the Value You Offer

The cornerstone for your success starts with ensuring your understanding of what successful lead generation really means. It is not the sleazy concept of dropping off a business card and then racing to someone else to repeat the process over and over again. That type of person merely wants you to hear about them. They offer no value.

Who would you rather have business dealings with—someone who is shallow like the guy who throws his business card in your face or someone who you view as a provider of value, who consistently offers you tips and with whom you've developed a level of comfort?

In today's digital world, relationship building and lead generation are all about the value of your offer to your target audience, and that requires a process to maximize its effectiveness. To be blunt, if this is not your idea of relationship building, don't even bother with LinkedIn.

Netiquette Is Important

There are many nuances to participating on various social networking sites, and they seem to change daily. Most of these sites are communities where people have invested long hours into participating. You may even say they've invested part of their lives into these sites. Given these investments, they don't take it lightly if someone jumps in and doesn't properly participate.

Consider the following in your participation:

- New to a function or group? Consider taking some time to get the lay of the land before jumping in to participate. Read what others are saying, check out the "power users," and make note of the tone being used.

- If you think you might be spamming, you probably should avoid the activity. Always have a reason for doing something on LinkedIn. Just randomly posting information for no good reason is spamming. Sending invitations to strangers is spamming. For instance, people try to connect with as many people as possible in their industry, even if they don't know them, by just hitting the invite button. LinkedIn frowns on that. Send invitations only to those with whom you have made a personal connection.

- In line with the point above, avoid sending a generic or default invitation or message—you know, the one that states "<insert name> would like to invite you..." If you send a personal note instead, you have a better chance of making that critical connection. **Always "add value,"** even if it is a simple little note to the person you are trying to connect with. Note: when using the current version (at the time of this writing) of the iPad, the option to provide a note is not available. It only sends a default invite.

- Treat every connection you make with respect. Remember, LinkedIn is a business community. Professional courtesy is the norm. Saying "please" and "thank you" is a good way to start. Even if you have no need to connect with someone, be polite when saying no.

Make yourself a valuable member of the LinkedIn community. Keep the following maxim in mind: "Few people who are either irrelevant or irritating on LinkedIn find any success." Remember, as we learned in Rule #4, *communicate the value your prospects are seeking and then you can get SALES!*

Consider the ROI

Measuring your ROI from social networking is difficult. The most effective way to measure ROI is to measure the tangibles.

As these rules begin to increase your "knowledge portfolio," let's take a quick look at how you might consider *measuring return on investment* (ROI) for your lead generation efforts.

ROI is a common measurement that evaluates the amount of benefit derived from an investment.

For instance, assume your digital networking investment consists of spending five hours per week on LinkedIn. Now, let's assume your time is worth two hundred dollars per hour. Across a year, your investment is roughly 50 thousand dollars! So, is it worth your time?

Well, this is where it gets gray. The problem is that when it comes to measuring the ROI, returns are not direct and immediate. Thus, the big question is, "How do you properly measure a return from your activities?"

Let's try to attack it from a financial analyst's standpoint. They are interested in annualized results (i.e., results that occur across a 12-month period). For example, assume in an average week, you connect with 10 *new* people in addition to following up with 20 *existing* contacts. Thus, by the end of the year, you can directly attribute, say, 30 thousand dollars of sales to your networking. Mathematically, for all your effort, your return looks like this: (($30,000 – $50,000)/$50,000) = -40 percent. Clearly, a *negative return* of 40 percent is an outright failure, right? As Lee Corso (from ESPN's *College Gameday*) likes to say, "Not so fast, my friend." Why?

Let's take a closer look.

First, while you have directly connected and followed up with people, you have undoubtedly also connected with an untold amount of people indirectly (friends of your connections, people who saw your communications but didn't communicate directly with you, etc.). There is no way to calculate what benefits these returned. At the very least, one nontangible benefit is establishing brand awareness for yourself. A more tangible but immeasurable benefit is that these "passive connections" more than likely contributed to your sales as well. Either way, this benefit is missing and can't be calculated, but it is still a benefit.

Second, the time it takes to build customer relationships varies. For some, the time is immediate, while others need to work through their "marketing funnel," which may take a year or longer. Thus, all those "long-termers" who take more than 12 months to show results (based on the calculation parameters above) are not captured either, but they too provide benefits.

The point is clear or, in this case, sort of a foggy gray that measuring your ROI from digital marketing is difficult. So, short of giving away a free car to everyone to encourage a direct response, is there anything to look at to determine if you are getting the "bang for your digital marketing buck"?

Perhaps the most effective way to measure an ROI tangibly is to measure the following:

- **Profile and company page traffic:** make it a weekly measurement and look for growth trends.

- **Growth in connections:** easy to quantify, but focus on growing "connections of value".

- **Credibility components:** expect an increase in the number of "authoritative elements" in your "profile"—on LinkedIn, this could include recommendations, endorsements, InMails received, and LinkedIn mentions.

- **Lead growth via your website:** this assumes you use LinkedIn to create awareness to your site. Look at "total" growth as well as observe the growth trend from month to month. Expect increasing amounts of opt-ins, the longer you continue using effective tactics.

Occam's Razor states, "All other things being equal, the simplest solution is the best." However, in this case, that doesn't fit. The simplest solution to measuring the ROI in digital marketing may be misleading. The astute marketer will include the above elements to provide the most effective measurement from the benefits of your lead generation endeavors.

7 What Does a LinkedIn Lead Look Like?

It is important to recognize what makes a good lead.

The goal of this second edition is to focus on the path toward generating results and using LinkedIn for leads. Clearly, LinkedIn offers a fertile ground for finding leads and nurturing these relationships to get paying customers. Its unmatched potential for lead generation lies in the unique opportunity it provides. It offers the opportunity to potentially communicate with vast amounts of decision-makers while having the incredible insight to see their professional backgrounds.

However, before spending potentially significant time and money developing these relationships, it is important to recognize what makes a good lead. Almost everyone in the sales world has their own definition of a sales lead. Within the context of LinkedIn, the following definition should be considered for a LinkedIn lead: you have a quality lead if you are communicating with someone from your target audience with full insight into their LinkedIn profile.

The Three Components of a LinkedIn Lead

1. You Should Be "Communicating" with Them

This is very important in determining if your contact is a LinkedIn lead. People use LinkedIn to gather and share industry-related information. Become part of that dialogue. There are numerous ways to do that, ranging from direct contact (e.g., e-mails, InMails, and comments) to indirect contacts (e.g., endorsements, "likes," and daily updates). One simple example might consist of sending personal notes to your contacts along with links to interesting articles and videos.

The following are important in terms of the communication process:

- **Communicate:** as basic as this sounds, the first step in defining a LinkedIn lead is to ensure that you are currently communicating with your contact.

- **Value:** clearly, you would want the contact to pay attention to your communication, and the best way to do that is to communicate something of value to your contact. For example, if they are looking to grow their marketing, offer something of value in line with that.

- **Frequency:** online communication is similar to a conversation. There are norms for the amount of communication that one can focus on. Be cognizant of not "over-communicating" or being pushy. Your frequency should have an appropriate mix of direct and indirect communication.

2. They Should Be Part of Your Target Audience

Be clear on knowing what your target audience looks like (note: this is the focus of Rule #9). The more detailed your definition, the better. That will let you know if your contact fits with the audience you are looking to communicate with. If the contact is not in that audience, or only a partial fit, that person is not a good lead to pursue. Ultimately, your company will not be offering what that person wants or needs.

3. Their Profiles Should Clearly Indicate That They Are Decision-Makers

The LinkedIn profile is literally a virtual persona for the person you are connected to. It is a proverbial marketer's gold mine with all kinds of information that helps one find common points to enhance the relationship-building process. It also helps you vet whether this person is a decision-maker or not. While communicating with an IT technician can give you company insight and a link inside, that person likely has no decision-making power. Ensure that you have this insight. It is a key component in the definition of a LinkedIn lead.

Next Steps

A good LinkedIn lead is a decision-maker from your target audience that you are communicating with. Take the time to evaluate your existing LinkedIn process, review your current contacts, and consider each person you come into contact with to decide if they are potential leads. In some cases, you may have some strong leads, and in other cases, you may have no connection whatsoever. Time is money. Focus on converting your LinkedIn contact into a LinkedIn lead, and then focus on turning that lead into a customer.

Section II
Strategize

LinkedIn is a communication platform. As with any platform you use, we advocate that you start by strategizing. It's all about having a focus and a purpose that aligns with your business. In this section, we help you effectively create your strategy.

Simply being on LinkedIn IS NOT a business strategy.

Rule 8: Understanding Purpose Is the Key to Lead Generation

Rule 9: Target Audience—Are My Clients on LinkedIn?

Rule 10: Effective Communication to Your Target Audience Requires Sound Bites

Rule 11: Preparing Your Profile for Lead Generation

Rule 12: Complete Your Strategy with Effective Use

8 Understanding Purpose Is the Key to Lead Generation

As we touched on in Rule #3, LinkedIn is a platform. You probably use other business platforms for things such as accounting, HR, and payroll. Do you simply turn those platforms on and expect them to generate the benefits you are looking for? Most likely not. You start with a strategy and build the platform to accomplish that strategy. With certain platforms, you may even invest hundreds of thousands of dollars to have consultants set it up effectively for you. Now think of LinkedIn. How many of us take the same approach to our use on this tool?

This is one of the most impactful pieces of advice in this entire book. You need to set your business goals and strategy. Simply being on LinkedIn **is not** a business strategy. Your goals should drive your entire presence.

Here are three points to consider in creating your strategy:

First point: *determine if LinkedIn is a good fit for your business.* Businesses that offer products or services for other businesses tend to do well by leveraging LinkedIn.

Second point: *make a list of what your business can achieve through the use of LinkedIn.* Here are some benefits to consider:

- **Finding new talent to hire, partner, or contract with.** LinkedIn is great for hiring people.

- **Using it as a tool for learning.** You can gain a great education through reading key articles that others post.

- **Build a virtual Rolodex of business partners and people you network with.** You can use LinkedIn to find people. You can search for those in a particular industry, location, or company quite easily. It is a great forum for connecting to those in your target market.

- **Demonstrate your credibility and experience.** As you will read in some of our other rules, this is key for people in terms of generating results.

- **A tool to keep communications flowing.** Sometimes, it is hard to keep up a verbal conversation with a partner or prospect. LinkedIn offers simple, non-intrusive ways to keep the communication flowing.

- **Identify key decision-makers and prospects for account entry points.** Look for ways to generate warm introductions based on your network. For companies you are looking to prospect with, look for connections or contacts within your network that can be connected to them.

- **Minimize cold calling.** LinkedIn offers a neat little function that shows, at a glance, what you and other LinkedIn members have in common.

Our suggestions are merely a drop in the bucket. Depending on your use of LinkedIn, there are many more benefits that you can, and will, tap into. Remember, the only limit to one's vision is one's vision.

Third Point: *understand the steps that make a lead generation process work well.*

- **Start with a strategy.** Build a great personal profile.

- **Create awareness.** Be consistently visible, and stay top-of-mind.

- **Engage your network.** Share interesting, valuable, helpful content with your network.

- **Convert.** Trust is created, and people tend to do business with those they trust.

In our LinkedIn methodology, we advocate you start by strategizing. This defines your overall business path to connect and grow with your target audience. Don't let this concept overwhelm you. It's about having a focus and a purpose when you use LinkedIn that aligns with your business. Think of it like this: if you want to travel from point A to point B, you can clearly define your route. Conversely, if you don't know where you want to travel to, you are probably going to simply wander endlessly and not get anywhere, which is unfortunately the fate of many millions of LinkedIn users.

9 Target Audience—Are My Clients on LinkedIn?

You should be where your prospects are.

Once you have your roadmap defined, you need to focus on communicating to those that are interested in what you offer, that is, your target audience. Not all of the millions of people on LinkedIn are potential customers; it is up to you to identify who they are and where they can be found. Ultimately, that will go a long way toward determining the value LinkedIn has for your business. For instance, if you sell businesses for a living, can you find business owners on LinkedIn that are looking to potentially sell their businesses?

Before you invest a great deal of time into your LinkedIn presence, do some quick research to learn about your target audience on LinkedIn.

1. **Clearly identify your ideal audience.**

   - Have a clear picture of the key attributes your clients have.

   - What is the size of the business you are targeting?

   - Who are the decision-makers in that business?

   - What are your clients buying from you?

   - What motivates them to buy from you?

   - How do they interact online?

   - What type of information might they be searching for to help them grow or solve a business problem?

   - What are the biggest problems they are trying to solve?

These are just some of the attributes that will drive what you do, from deciding what online and offline networks to involve yourself in, to targeting who you ultimately decide to prospect.

2. **Perform some quick searches to find your audiences.**

- **Follow your competitors to see where they participate.** This is pretty self-explanatory and also probably the easiest way.

- **Simply ask the people you do business with.** Talk to people you know are in the industry, and see if they are on LinkedIn. If they are on LinkedIn, check how they use the site. If they take part in groups, join those groups.

- **Search LinkedIn for groups that relate to your business.** LinkedIn has groups that have become the go-to place for industry leaders to gather for discussions on relevant topics.

- **Create a company page for your business, and see who follows it.** If people in your industry are active on LinkedIn, they are looking for companies like yours. When people start following your company, look at their profile and company pages. This will give you more intel on where people that are interested in your business can be found.

- **Search company pages for the types of companies you do business with.** You may know the industry-leading companies in your industry. Look for what kind of presence they have on LinkedIn. Look for executives and managers from those companies, and see how they take part.

3. **Once found, begin to interact and gain recognition.**

As you start finding your target audience, as soon as you are comfortable, begin to interact with them. For instance, if you found a specific industry group, join it. (Note: while some of these groups might be closed to the public, many will be open to all LinkedIn users.) Watch how the group communicates, and use that as a guide to becoming visible in the group. Post insightful questions, and answer some as well. Don't be blatantly self-promotional. Sharing your knowledge through valuable content is especially important because it builds trust and helps current and potential connections assess whether you're someone who is worth their time.

Closing Thought

The old business cliché is "chase the green, not the dream." Paraphrasing this for a marketing context, "you should be where your prospects are." In the online world, many executive decision-makers and business people are on LinkedIn. Now, it is up to you to find and connect with them.

10 Effective Communication to Your Target Audience Requires Sound Bites

Susan Harrow's
Success

Have you ever heard of the Oprah effect? It's where an endorsement from Oprah can suddenly turn a small business into a multimillion-dollar company. This has been such a powerful phenomenon that CNBC focused an entire hour-long special exploring it. One of the people they interviewed during this show was Susan Harrow, media coach and consultant (www.PRsecrets.com), who wrote a book called *The Ultimate Guide to Getting Booked on Oprah*.[3]

While our 42 rules are not focused on getting on the Oprah show, they are focused on generating results on LinkedIn. The process Susan laid out in her book has very strong applications for us to connect with our target audiences on LinkedIn. In Susan's book, Oprah was the target audience. The first step Susan discussed focused on getting to know Oprah, her background, her philosophy, and what shapes her show. We should focus on a similar first step as we begin to communicate with our target audiences.

The next step is an incredibly powerful one. We need to establish the ability to get our message out, via a targeted sound bite, to our desired audience. We love Susan's extreme example of taking the full story of war and peace and communicating it in a haiku. To be effective in today's busy digital world, if we are unable to communicate value in a sound bite, we might not have a chance to communicate anything at all.

---

[3] Susan Harrow, *The Ultimate Guide to Getting Booked on Oprah: Ten Steps to Becoming a Guest on the World's Top Talk Show* (Oakland, CA: Harrow Communications, 2003).

The "Sound Bite Queen"

In many ways, Susan has carried over the impacts of the Oprah effect into her LinkedIn activities, and these have generated multiple successes for her. Successes have ranged from generating new sales to new business partnerships to fun experiences, which don't result in bottom-line impacts but offer fabulous life encounters. Given that our target audience is a business professional looking for success on LinkedIn, we asked Susan about some of her tangible business successes on LinkedIn.

Susan is actively sought out on LinkedIn and has built up a network of contacts in the thousands. Interestingly, many people seek her out for her info products related to media training and PR, even if she doesn't deliver those services live herself. Given this interest, Susan has created a solid revenue stream communicating through regular LinkedIn e-mails. While the impact from this is much more modest, in certain ways, it is analogous to the effect Oprah had by communicating through your TV screen. Oprah was known for helping her audience by connecting them to great things and guiding people to "live [their] best life."[4] In a sense, Susan is doing the same by offering her connections ways to better their business.

In one of her most recent e-mail campaigns, she generated a CTR (click-through rate) of a little north of 10 percent but had conversions of 70 percent who made a purchase. This results in a strong five-figure check. Why do people purchase from her? They want the ability to learn to speak more effectively to their target audience and have results that are quickly impactful to their businesses.

Susan's Tips

1. When people take the time to write you something wonderful and original, make sure you write back. It will increase your engagement and lead to a higher one-on-one relationship.

2. Always think in terms of sound bites. We live in a three-second world. If your subject doesn't catch interest in less than three seconds, you've lost them.

3. Consider the following when addressing your target audience: What does my audience need to know now and how can I help? Package your phrasing to support that. Your goal is to match the intersection of your skills with their needs.

*Download "4 Simple Steps to Get on the Today Show Tomorrow"
to help jump-start your media interview success at
www.LeadGen2020.com/prsecrets.*

---

[4] "Oprah Winfrey's Official Website – Live Your Best Life – Oprah.com," Oprah.com, accessed August 2013, http://www.oprah.com.

11 Your Profile Communicates for You 24 Hours a Day

Limited activity on your profile means limited chances for generating leads.

We've established the need to find your target audience on LinkedIn with the goal being to tap into significant amounts of people interested in what you are selling. Well, that's actually the first part of the goal. They are the people you clearly want to connect with. The second part of that goal is making sure that you have an effective LinkedIn presence in place to greet your target audience whenever and wherever they find you. The main point in this presence is your profile. Addressing your profile is such a large topic that we will provide an overview of it in this rule but devote an entire section (Section III) to it for more detail.

When LinkedIn cracked the two-hundred-million-user mark, it celebrated by sending congratulatory notes to users they deemed as the "Top 1%, 5%, or 10%." The measurements used were not clear, but based on anecdotal information, it would seem that 90 percent of the LinkedIn world has relatively little activity on their profile.

Limited activity on your profile means limited chances for generating leads. That is a tough pill to swallow given that your profile is a billboard for you. It communicates for you 24 hours a day. You have the ability to express your unique selling proposition—effectively telling others why they need to do business with you. Now, understand the parameters this must be done in—you will generally get no more than a glance, perhaps only three seconds, to catch someone's attention.

Let's flip this around a moment and focus on your perspective when you read profiles. If you read someone's profile that is pretty basic, do you spend time on it or simply move on? Most people will simply move on. A user with this type of profile has already **lost** before they've begun. Your profile is a business asset. It is something to be refined and respected as it will represent you 24 hours a day, seven days a week.

Let's touch on some quick things you should consider (and there are more in Section III):

1. **LinkedIn "rates" your profile.** Let's start there. If you are not rated an "all-star," click on the link to "improve your profile strength" and address those items. Doing this is very beneficial, but it is simply one component of what needs to be done.

2. **Personalize your profile.** Once you've addressed all of the main profile components, refine them. For instance, with the summary, start with a powerful one-line heading. Then create a rich summary of your background. Don't just tell your audience what you did; tell them why you did it.

3. **Rearrange your profile to highlight what's important first.** Based on our current research, this doesn't appear to be something that's commonly done, but you can actually rearrange your LinkedIn profile so that certain sections come before others. It can be a big benefit for you to highlight your strongest elements to your profile first (remember, people tend to only give you a glance).

4. **It is important to properly promote your profile.** If no one sees it, how will they know about you? (For more, see Rule #17.)

If your profile page is not filled out to its fullest form and instantly recognizable as your brand, your ability to generate leads will suffer. Before sharing any content or trying the strategies discussed, be sure that your profile is maximized. Remember, what do you do when you come to a weak profile? You leave almost immediately.

12 Complete Your Strategy with Effective Use

An account does not equal immediate results.

Everyone wants to effectively use LinkedIn, so why do most of us have trouble with that? You may be thinking right now that you have a good strategy and some solid tactics for attracting people to your profile or company page, but is this enough to be effective? Let's review some of the things that help maximize your effective use of LinkedIn.

Focus on your business path and goal. In one of the first rules in this book, you were asked the questions, "Why are you on LinkedIn?" and "What are you looking to achieve?" Your answers to those questions should help you build out your purpose for using LinkedIn. This is the cornerstone for leveraging the site for lead generation. The fact is that the large majority of users fail to realize the potential for using this tool. If you have reached this point and do not have a "roadmap" to follow, stop here and work on it before continuing. Effective use of LinkedIn requires articulating a purpose and pursuing it.

Maximize your profile *before* participating. As we just learned in Rule #11, this is your virtual neon sign. Make it very engaging!

No spamming, bragging, or selling. Pretty straightforward. Make sure you add value versus simply promoting yourself. As noted in Rule #5, few people who are either irrelevant or irritating on LinkedIn find any success.

Avoid haphazard participation. This is not rocket science, but it is very important to adhere to it. Unfortunately, many people join and collect contacts but invest no time or energy networking, so they gain nothing from the site. Make sure you sustain your participation—don't post sometimes and not others. Think of this like a conversation. As long as you are talking to someone, people remain to listen. Once you stop talking, they leave. Don't let them leave.

Manage your expectations. Nothing is a bigger buzzkill than not meeting your expectations, which, quite bluntly, many fail to do on LinkedIn. People that effectively use LinkedIn set their expectations appropriately (e.g., contributing to conversations, gaining endorsements, and generating more profile views). These people don't shoot for the moon, and when they miss, they don't quit. They realize an account does not immediately equal results. They know it takes time and set their expectations accordingly. Remember, little successes create bigger ones.

Make your effort manageable. Everyone is busy, yet many still find ways to generate success on LinkedIn. This is because they set their paths to be manageable—perhaps 15 minutes a day on most days but sometimes more. Remember, LinkedIn is just a tool to connect and open doors, but it still takes work on your part to make it effective. Your goal is to set and sustain the proper amount of daily participation.

Don't bet all your chips on one tactic. Have you noticed that there are a variety of tactics that work best when they work together? Generally speaking, they all need to be integrated to have an effective flow to LinkedIn—if one of them is out of whack, your chances for success can be greatly minimized.

Offer items of significance on a sustained basis to your target audience. Think about this like you would a commercial on TV. What are the odds that you make a purchase from viewing one commercial? Probably slim to none. Why? Because you have no connection or relationship to the item being sold. The advertiser needs to plan out their message, determine where they can most effectively find his or her target audience, schedule the time to run the commercials, and, most importantly, run the advertisements on a consistent basis. Once a relationship is created, the advertiser's odds for success increase dramatically.

Section III
Profile

Your personal profile is like your personal billboard. You never know who is going to see it, but for those who do read it, you want it to exude as much beneficial information about you as possible. It speaks on your behalf 24 hours a day, seven days a week. The focus of this section is to help you increase the overall effectiveness of your profile.

Rule 13: Generating Awareness Off LinkedIn Can Drive Big Results on LinkedIn

Rule 14: Preparing Your Profile for Lead Generation

Rule 15: Give Yourself a Fast, Powerful Makeover!

Rule 16: You Are Your Brand!

Rule 17: Promote Your Profile

Rule 18: Integrate Your Profile to Drive Multiple Marketing Elements

Rule 19: Take Control of Your LinkedIn Experience

13 Generating Awareness Off LinkedIn Can Drive Big Results on LinkedIn

Bruce Rector's Success

The old joke asks, "What school should I attend to get the best business vision?" The answer is, "The school for high-rise window washers." Obviously, the context is that a person can see farther and with greater clarity from the outside of a tall building than the average person can standing flat-footed on the ground.

We would like to introduce you to someone who should be teaching business vision at this "special school." It's not just because he has attended some of the most prestigious institutions for higher learning but because his career has always been focused on providing leading-edge growth strategies, initially to his employers and, over the last decade or so, to his clients and readers. His name is Bruce Rector, and he is the president of the Rector Group (www.TheRectorGroup.com), a consulting practice that focuses on providing high-quality strategy and corporate finance services to middle-market companies.

Bruce shares his vision through his business column with the *South Florida Business Journal*, something he has been doing for a number of years. Bruce has always been a great "traditional" networker. Early on, he had the vision to jump in and be an early adopter of both LinkedIn and business social networking. It is through the combination of his business column and LinkedIn networking that Bruce has realized his biggest LinkedIn successes.

Awareness Plus Credibility Equals Revenue

Business is constantly evolving, and Bruce stays on top of these changes while writing on topics that have ranged from business strategy to corporate governance topics and corporate finance. Many of Bruce's columns have been picked up by sister *Business Journal* publications around the country, which have certainly been very helpful in elevating his profile and generating awareness to his business.

As we've been learning throughout this book, one of the most significant elements for generating results on LinkedIn starts with generating awareness to your LinkedIn profile. It doesn't matter whether you generate this awareness directly on LinkedIn or off it, but, either way, you are able to effectively direct it to where you can generate your greatest business value. This is exactly what Bruce has experienced.

People read his articles and are sufficiently impressed to take the time to look him up on LinkedIn. His profile was created and aligned with his website so one can act as a conduit for the other.

In one particular situation, he was fortunate that an entrepreneur came across one of his columns. Intrigued by what she read, she decided to check his "credibility" on LinkedIn. After reviewing his profile several times, she ultimately made her way to The Rector Group website. This site is continually adding various types of new content, so it is quite robust with business insight. Sufficiently satisfied with her research, she requested a consult with Bruce, which led to an extensive engagement involving finance, organizational design, and market analyses to support the launch of a new company in the cosmetics industry space.

Bruce's Tips

1. **Awareness.** Strategically consider all the avenues available to you to generate awareness, and then make sure your LinkedIn profile intersects them all.

2. **Your profile.** This literally speaks for you and your business 24 hours a day, seven days a week. It is the most cost-effective "sales resource" you can ever have. Make sure you maximize your profile!

3. **Content.** Everyone knows that content is king, but be strategic in how it is used. Consider the SEO impact, the human impact, and how it strategically fits within your business strategy.

Sign up at, www.LeadGen2020.com/rector, and receive a free business challenge each week. Or download his free eBook, 5 Tips Every Entrepreneur Should Know.

14 Preparing Your Profile for Lead Generation

LinkedIn claims that users with complete profiles are 40 times more likely to receive opportunities on LinkedIn.

Think of the profile like you would a dinner table at a big family gathering. When people show up, they expect the table to be filled with food, and they expect to sit around it for hours talking. If there is no food, expectations haven't been met, and, more than likely, no one is going to spend significant time around that table.

Since the profile is so important in the "roadmap to results" on LinkedIn, we've decided to build upon Rule #11 and provide additional suggestions for you to consider. Let's start at the beginning and focus this rule on completing your profile. Unfortunately, too many people think that just by having a profile on LinkedIn, they'll get business.

Completing Your Profile

Regrettably, many people try to do the barest of the basics and hope that generates them new business. By now, it is clear why it won't. If your page is not filled out to its fullest form and instantly recognizable as your brand, your effectiveness will suffer. Before sharing any content or trying the strategies discussed, at the very least, you need to make sure your profile is "complete." LinkedIn claims that users with complete profiles are 40 times more likely to receive opportunities on LinkedIn. If you were ever wondering what attributes constitute a "complete profile," they are:

• Your industry and location

• An up-to-date current position (with a description)

• Two past positions

- Your education
- Your skills (minimum of three)
- A profile photo
- At least 50 connections

Notice how LinkedIn has evolved. When the first edition of this book came out, LinkedIn encouraged each user to add their "specialties." Now, that has been replaced with "skills," which lead to endorsements (which we talk about in Rule #32). Clearly, they've created a much more interactive process.

Also, LinkedIn originally focused on generating three recommendations. While this started out as a very powerful idea, it very quickly became abused by people generating recommendations from people they didn't even know. Even worse, it bogged down profiles by having a list of recommendations smack in the middle. The more recommendations you had, the harder you made it for people to want to scroll through your entire profile. In the most current iteration of LinkedIn, recommendations have been more neatly integrated into the profile but have also been de-emphasized in this revision.

Other Profile-Related Insight

Updating and revising your profile. Whenever you make changes to your profile, you need to select the "edit" link (which is either to the right or left) for **each** of the major categories on your profile (e.g., summary and education) and then follow the directions.

You may be aware that when you make a substantial change to your profile (e.g., by adding a new current job, school, or website), your entire network receives an alert. You can control whether your connections receive updates. As of this writing, this is achieved by navigating to "profile updates" on the "account & settings" page.

Your photograph. As the saying goes, a picture is worth a thousand words. Adding your photograph to LinkedIn allows you to create another connection with anyone visiting your profile. A nice, professional headshot is the best choice, but any professional-looking photograph will do. When you add a photo, it shows a different level of commitment to using the LinkedIn tool. Given the fact that we're visually oriented, adding anything that enhances your profile is a definite plus. You have complete control over who sees your photo on LinkedIn. In fact, you have access to three levels of privacy. You can allow your direct connections, your network, or everyone access to your photo.

15 Give Yourself a Fast, Powerful Makeover!

Updating your professional headline is something that offers an incredible ROI in terms of benefit gained versus time spent.

For most people, their LinkedIn experience begins with an invitation from someone they know. It is probably the curiosity factor that gets them to initially register with LinkedIn. We actually took a little nonscientific survey, and curiosity was overwhelmingly indicated as the impetus for registering.

While curiosity is an impetus, it is not one that is overwhelming. Thus, people tend to go through the signup process as quickly as possible, usually not completely filling out their profile as no one likes to spend unnecessary time signing up on another one of these ubiquitous websites. Unfortunately, by racing through this, they also tend to overlook one of the most important elements to their LinkedIn success. During the registration process, one of the very first things someone needs to do is to create their professional headline. It may be subtle, but it is important, yet most people quickly skip past it addressing it only with the bare minimal requirement.

Think about this. Do you realize that many times when your name appears on LinkedIn, your professional headline also appears? Your name could come up in a search or within someone's network or in the list of people you may know, but the bottom line is that your name and professional headline very often show up together. Essentially, this headline functions as your three-second brand statement or your three-second bumper sticker.

Let's illustrate the power of this with a little example: Which of these headlines is more powerful?

John Doe (20-year expert facilitating $100,000,000 in high-tech mergers)

or

Bob Doe (Owner, Doe & Associates)

Clearly, the first professional headline is more functional and quickly enables you to understand what John Doe does and where his key strength lies.

Now, let's look at a practical implication of the two headlines above. Let's say you are doing a search on "high-tech mergers." Assume both John Doe and Bob Doe have the right keywords in their profiles and they alone show up in the search. When you look at the search results, all you are able to see is a name and the professional description. Think about it, who are you going to be drawn to in a list of names, John or Bob Doe? It is very likely you will at least check out John because he tells you he is an expert in high-tech mergers, while Bob doesn't tell you anything of relevance.

We spoke to a group of "C-level" business people discussing the value of a LinkedIn profile. To illustrate this point, we presented an individual's profile piecemeal. First, we highlighted his five hundred plus connections. Next, we showed his vanity link, which made it easy to find his profile. Following this, we showed his links directing traffic to his blog and website. Then we asked, "Is this a maximized profile?" Most heads nodded. So, we finally showed his professional description, which was very vague and bland and asked if anyone in the room knew what this individual did. Since it was so nondescript, no one understood what this individual's expertise was. Now we asked again, "Was this a maximized profile?" This time, the answer was a resounding no. The moral of the story is, "Activity is not achievement." In this age of multitasking and business at the speed of light, no matter how many people you connect with, if people can't quickly ascertain your business value, the odds of them seeking to do business with you rapidly diminish.

While we call it a 30-second makeover, whatever it takes you to do, it is absolutely worth the investment of your time. Updating your professional headline is something that offers an incredible ROI in terms of benefit gained versus time spent. Invest in yourself, and quickly show the world your expertise and project your brand!

You Are Your Brand!

Each of us projects our brand through everything we do, wear, touch, or discuss.

There are millions and millions of registered users on LinkedIn. Given that sheer volume, how are you going to get people to find you, and, more importantly, when they do find you, are you projecting the right brand that will help your chances for success?

Let's start by asking, "What is your brand?" Whether we acknowledge it or not, each of us projects our brand through everything we do, wear, touch, or discuss. Therefore, as many famous marketers have said, "You are your brand." We've compiled a list of things you can do to enhance your brand and improve your ability to "exhibit" it on LinkedIn:

- Make effective use of your professional headline (see Rule #15).

- In your summary, make sure the top two lines clearly articulate your value. This works on two levels. First, it gives someone reading your profile an immediate overview of your value. Secondly, this works outside of LinkedIn too. These two lines are currently being picked up on Bing as your "bio" within their search. Hence, someone searching your name on Bing will see the first two lines of your summary describing you.

- Maximize your company profile (or, if you don't have one yet, set one up). This is a distinctly different use of branding than you have available to you on your personal profile (see Rule #31).

- Post items of value that your target audience will derive significance from and exhibit your expertise. Need help finding topics? Set up a Google Alert around a keyword or phrase (e.g., digital marketing), and you will receive e-mails delivered directly into your inbox with articles and blog posts from around the web.

- Use the inShare sharing feature currently found on most articles on the web. Within seconds, you can share information on your activity stream, with your groups, with your Twitter link, or with anyone in your network (see Rule #36).

- Show your expertise, and share value as your target audience defines it.

- Add your LinkedIn profile URL to your e-mail signature and business card.

- LinkedIn Answers no longer exists, but people are always posting questions. Look for connections' questions on LinkedIn and answer them. Follow up to make sure they got what they needed.

- When you invite someone to get LinkedIn to you, personalize the note.

- Link your blog back to your LinkedIn profile.

- Prepare ahead of time and read the blogs or check out the websites of key people that you communicate with.

- Consider starting a LinkedIn group around a specific topic that relates to your brand. While it is easy to start a group, growing a group requires the same methodology you are currently reading about (strategy, awareness, engagement, and conversion).

- Use a specific name (relevant to your brand) to name your links (e.g., OperationsGuru.com versus My Blog).

- Don't lie, don't pitch, and don't spam. Your brand should be that of providing value, not snake oil.

- (Bonus) Be confident!

There are certainly a bunch more tips to add, and we welcome them all. Feel free to share this list or leave comments with your own tips at www.LeadGen2020.com/tips. All the best to developing your future success stories!

Promote Your Profile

Your profile is a billboard for you.

Your LinkedIn profile displays *your brand,* and it is the starting point of your LinkedIn experience. It is one of your most important elements on LinkedIn. It's the place where you will summarize all of your professional endeavors, including your employment, website, awards, certifications, background information, education, and interests. It's also where you can post your photograph, adding another way to connect with others. Your profile is visible to the people who are included in your network—the people with whom you've directly connected. You should consider it a work in progress as you continually update it to increase its effectiveness.

Your Profile Is a Billboard for You

Think of your profile like a billboard—you never know who is going to see it, but for those who do read it, you want it to be as effective as possible. LinkedIn actually lets you know who has read your profile. Have you ever noticed that little text box on the right side of your LinkedIn home page that states, "Your profile has been viewed by 12 people in the last five days. In the last three days, you have appeared in search results 89 times"?

If you are not seeing numbers in that range, then let's start focusing on what you could be doing to promote your profile.

Promoting Your Profile

- **Communicate your profile link.** When you have a LinkedIn profile, make sure it becomes part of your marketing efforts. A very simple and quick way to promote your profile is to create a vanity link and add it to your e-mail signature. Perhaps say something like this: *Want to connect with me on LinkedIn? Please visit www.LinkedIn.com/In/John Doe.* Be sure it is on your business cards. Don't forget to add it to your website. Also, you may want to consider sending a personalized message out to your connections letting them know about your presence on LinkedIn. All of these will spread the word.

- **Invite people.** Another straightforward way to promote your profile is accomplished simply through inviting more people to connect. Don't spam. Focus this on people you know or whom you have something in common with. Once they receive the invitation, they can accept and then view your profile.

- **Optimize for external search.** Be cognizant about how you write your profile as public profiles currently receive a very strong weighting with the search engines. Be sure to optimize your profile for search engines. Fill out your profile completely. Expand your network of LinkedIn contacts. Participate in groups. All of these raise your profile in search engine results.

- **Use LinkedIn PPC.** LinkedIn ads work in the pay-per-click model. You bid on certain words, and the highest bidders get highest placement. These ads are great for generating interest in your internal profile and groups you might start (see Rule #28).

- **Groups.** Participation in groups is integral to developing your awareness to your presence on LinkedIn. Actively participate in groups that relate to your brand and are effectively moderated (see Rule #33).

Many business owners set up a presence on LinkedIn because other companies and business owners have done the same. But, once it is up and running, they do nothing else with it. That is a costly mistake.

A basic profile will not get you the attention you want. Making your profile the best possible must get on the top of your to-do list. You need to refine it and respect it. It represents your business 24 hours a day, seven days a week, 365 days a year. Maximize your profile before you begin trying to raise awareness of it. Go back to it routinely to tweak it and freshen up the content.

18 Integrate Your Profile to Drive Multiple Marketing Elements

Gaida Zirkelbach's Success

In 2009, Chris was invited to speak to a group of roughly two hundred interactive marketers at the W Hotel in Fort Lauderdale. The topic was "LinkedIn: Business & Personal Success Strategies." As part of his presentation, he chose a person from the group ahead of time and offered her suggestions for a "LinkedIn profile makeover." She went ahead and implemented these, and Chris shared "before" and "after" screenshots of her profile during his talk. The person he worked with was Gaida Zirkelbach, shareholder at Gunster, Florida's law firm for business, as they are known.

Watching the Seeds Sprout

We recently checked in with Gaida to see how things have been working out, and she had a lot to share with us. To be clear, we are not taking any credit for the results Gaida has achieved. All of the credit belongs to her. We simply shared some suggestions and did a little coaching, and she ran with the rest.

Tactically, we initially worked on the main elements of her profile (e.g., headline, summary, and experience). Strategically, we discussed different elements of LinkedIn, their impacts, and how she could potentially generate more awareness and engagement. After that, Gaida ran with this, integrating it with her entire social media business approach.

Her ability to integrate LinkedIn with her other online interactions makes a powerful combination, and she shared some of what she did. For instance, she used similar language to what she put on her

LinkedIn profile across Twitter, SlideShare, and her law firm's website bio. She also created a Pinterest page, a Google Plus page and +1'd articles, and other things that she wanted to highlight. As a result, when she Googles her name, prospects see what she wants them to, with her LinkedIn page consistently coming up as the second or third result.

The Multiple Elements of LinkedIn Success

Let's fast forward to her results. She has received multiple cold calls from potential clients without having to do any other networking, and at least two of those cold calls in the last two years have become good, paying clients.

However, let's also rewind a moment. While we tend to talk in terms of absolute results, that is, "he or she sold a 25-thousand-dollar contract," typically, there is a process of smaller results that occurs before any business results. Gaida shared some of her experiences.

Her target audiences are entrepreneurs, CEOs, and in-house counsel. Thus, she targeted language in her profile to those individuals, which was also integrated into her other social channels as well. Through this approach, she has been able to:

- Connect with key business prospects, many of which have turned into clients as a result of a bigger marketing effort and connections, but LinkedIn played a significant part

- Connect with a world-renowned entrepreneur and speaker and get him to speak to a group of clients and prospects, thus leveraging LinkedIn to make connections that she can then use for further marketing events

- Use LinkedIn to research individuals she is meeting with or even opposing counsel

Gaida's Tips

1. Make sure that your profile sends the right message. Step back and look at it from a prospect's point of view. Are you using the right keywords and making it clear that you can help them?

2. Make the most of your profile. Use it to research individuals, make connections, see who looks at your profile, keep in touch, and reach out when a contact makes a career change.

3. Promote your profile, and use it to promote you and your experience. Add a link to your profile in your e-mail signature lines, link out to your bio or website from it, link to it, or use similar language to it on other social media channels.

Gaida helps entrepreneurs and in-house counsel with business, technology, Internet/social media, and privacy legal issues. Learn more at www.linkedin.com/in/gaida.

Take Control of Your LinkedIn Experience

Manage your settings.

LinkedIn is a powerful tool for making business connections, but it is just that—a tool. Even the most active users miss some simple ways to optimize the way they use LinkedIn. In the last of our profile-related rules, we are going to review the settings that drive your account. (Note: we are describing the settings as they exist in May 2013.)

You can create your personal URL by looking toward the top right of your LinkedIn screen and clicking on the little down arrow next to your name. Then click on "settings." As an additional security measure, it asks you to re-sign in, and after you do so, you arrive at the dashboard of your account settings.

On the top left, you should see your photo and the date you first became a member. Underneath that, you will see your primary e-mail address you've attached to your account. Quick tip: use a personal e-mail as your primary e-mail. If you use a business e-mail and you subsequently lose access to it (e.g., you leave the company), you may also lose your profile too. No e-mail, no profile access.

Toward the middle right on the top of your page, you can see how many InMails (see Rule #27) you have available and when your next grant is going to occur. To the far right, you will see a small list of frequently asked questions. Over the years, we've found these to be pretty solid and would suggest you become familiar with using them.

On the bottom left, in a tabbed layout, you have the four main "settings" for your account:

Profile tab. This is the first tab. In this section, you can control how you broadcast your activity and who can see it, select who can see your connections, and choose how you want to appear to others when you view their profile (i.e., your name and headline or somewhat anonymous showing just your industry and title or completely anonymous). One of the most important things that you can do in this section is edit your "public profile." This is how you appear when people search for you on Google, Yahoo!, Bing, etc.

Communication tab. This is located directly under the profile tab and focused on your e-mail experience within the site. While this may seem pretty generic, it is worthwhile to review. This section enables you to select the types of messages you receive, types of invitations you accept, the frequency of e-mails you get, and more.

Groups, companies, and applications tab. As the name of the tab suggests, this section focuses on these three LinkedIn elements, along with privacy controls, as they apply to third-party applications and plugins. Perhaps one non-intuitive thing to note as it relates to your old "LinkedIn apps" is that they've been replaced with features that let you display samples of your work on your profile. With it, you can link to or upload images, presentations, videos, or documents.

Account tab. In this change, you can manage your privacy as it relates to advertising preferences. You can manage your profile photo and visibility and customize the type of updates you see on your homepage. The current default shows 10 different types. If you don't want to receive some of those, with a click of a button you can hide whatever you don't want to see. Among other things, if you ever wondered how to close an account on LinkedIn, that function is listed under this setting.

Your profile is important from both a strategic and tactical perspective. Spend some time familiarizing yourself with key settings in your account. Understanding how those impact you can help you build a more effective roadmap for results.

Section IV
Attract

If your goal on LinkedIn is to generate business and leads, you need to think about growing your connections.

Get people interested in you. Stay relevant and don't become a spammer. Look for ways to make new connections while staying top-of-mind with your existing ones. Always focus on adding value. In this section, we are going to dig deeper into specific ways to help you generate positive awareness.

Rule 20: Make It Easy for People to Find You

Rule 21: Success Is Doing Something Simple That Turns into Something Special

Rule 22: Content Drives Awareness

Rule 23: Content Marketing—Making the Intangible Tangible

Rule 24: Learning How a LinkedIn "Like" Can Generate a Lead

Rule 25: Generate Awareness by Making It Easy to Be Found

Rule 26: Effective Awareness through Invites

Rule 27: Don't Overlook InMails because They Cost Money

Rule 28: There Are Immediate Paid Ways to Generate Leads Too

20 Make It Easy for People to Find You

Quality matters here. 50 quality contacts are infinitely more valuable to you than five hundred people you really don't communicate with.

Building your "roadmap to results" requires effort. The more time and effort you put in, the greater the potential value you can create. Strategically speaking, at this point you've set your business focus, identified your target audience, maximized your profile, and are itching to generate results. What's next? It's now all about generating positive awareness (i.e., traffic) to your profile. After all, if people don't know you exist, how can they do business with you?

Quality matters here. 50 quality contacts are infinitely more valuable to you than five hundred people you really don't communicate with. LinkedIn says that it's not about connections for connection's sake, and we agree. Building awareness is going to take some thought. The quality of your awareness should not be measured numerically.

If your goal is to generate business and leads on LinkedIn, you need to **think about growing your connections.** There are many different ways to connect, from meeting people offline to connecting with them on Facebook or Twitter. Think about peers in your industry, clients, prospective clients, community leaders, etc.—anybody you may know and have a good reason to be connected with.

Simple Ways to Begin Setting Up Your Roadmap for Awareness

- **Create your own LinkedIn "vanity link" (i.e., your own personal URL).** Every LinkedIn profile has a unique URL automatically created.

This includes the LinkedIn domain name followed by a stream of random letters and numbers—definitely not easy to remember. An attractive feature of LinkedIn is that you can personalize this URL using your name (if it's not already taken) or other identifying words, such as the name of your company. For example, Albert Einstein might have created a personal LinkedIn URL that looked like this: www.LinkedIn.com/in/AlbertEinstein.

- **Think about how you "find" people.** A very simple way is to reconnect online with people you know, that is, former colleagues or classmates. Dig into your past when filling in your profile. The more you include, the better your chances of being found by people you've previously associated with. In your profile, include past companies, education, affiliations, activities, etc. Conversely, be proactive, send an invitation, and add a quick blurb inside the invite to help reestablish the connection you previously had with that person.

- **Provide value/be a trusted source.** You want to be visible and show your business value. It takes time to achieve this. Studies have shown that it takes someone at least seven exposures to you before they really start to pay attention, listen, and determine whether it makes sense to take the next step.

- **Offline.** We all spend a lot of time thinking of ways to generate awareness *online,* but don't neglect the *offline* world. Integrate it every chance you can. Add your LinkedIn vanity link to your business card or e-mail signature.

Let's try to tie all of these tips together with an example. Let's say you meet and connect with someone at an industry trade show. You discussed the emerging trend in widget sales. As soon as you can, connect with them on LinkedIn. In your invitation, mention you were happy to talk with them about widget sales at the trade show. Now you have a new connection, and the beauty of LinkedIn is that it enables permission-based communication with your connections. Thus, you are able to remain top-of-mind without being annoying.

Maximize Awareness

Get people interested in you. Stay relevant and don't become a spammer. Look for ways to make new connections and always focus on adding value. In the next few rules, we are going to dig deeper into specific ways to generate positive awareness.

21 Success Is Doing Something Simple That Turns into Something Special

Des Walsh's Success: perform an action a day. Sustained small steps can ultimately lead to big successes.

Are you doing enough on LinkedIn? What is enough? What if you performed an action a day, six days a week, for 30 days? That was a question pondered by Des Walsh (www.DesWalsh.com), which ultimately became the seed for a global movement that is spreading LinkedIn success around the world!

When you first hear about the idea, it has an almost immediate attraction to it—so simple, yet so powerful. My first reaction? I instantly thought of the movie *Forrest Gump*, specifically the part where he just decided to run and didn't stop.[5] He ran from one coast to the other and back again. Since he was sustaining something so simple for so long, people saw something magical in it, and it attracted a large group that continued to grow and grow. While Des might not be running from coast to coast (or the Australian Outback as he is from Down Under), he is running his brainchild, the 30 Day Linking Blitz, and it is continuing to attract people to it from all over the world.

The Sparks of an Idea Lead to a Wildfire of Success

Ironically, this idea started because Des thought he wasn't doing enough on LinkedIn, even though he spends upward of an hour a day on the site.

---

[5] *Forrest Gump*, directed by Steven Spielberg (1994; Hollywood, CA: Paramount Pictures, 2001), DVD.

So he created a simple project for himself to do more each day. Once he did that, he thought it would be nice to have a few colleagues to do it with him. Soon, the word spread, and the group has grown rapidly to over 350 people from all across the globe.

Since its origin, the group has added some basic structure to help increase its impact. It is a 30-day program for people to improve their presence and engagement on LinkedIn. Participation is voluntary and requires only that you are a self-starter. Commitment should be for about 20 minutes per day focusing on a range of tasks across 30 days. To encourage success, there is a group environment that is very supportive. Besides offering this encouragement, the group dynamic is also a very strong relationship-building tool as well.

Participants have found real value in doing something on a consistent basis. They've seen tangible results through growing connections, increasing their presence, and attracting new leads. One participant stated, "The best part of the 30-Day Linking Blitz is that it doesn't end after 30 days. I walked away with tools to incorporate into my daily routine that will serve me well beyond the initial time investment."[6]

For Des, success on LinkedIn is being found by the people you want to find you and having that turn into the remunerative business activity or job you are seeking. It has been said that Des has been the provider of immense guidance on LinkedIn, and that didn't start happening yesterday. After all, he wrote one of the first books published on the topic of LinkedIn back in 2006.

Des' Tips

1. Start with the business basics. Ask yourself whom you are wanting to attract and what products or services do you offer that would be of interest to them.

2. Take a very hard look at your profile and company page. Get others to look at them as well and provide you feedback. The goal is to create a presence that is going to excite the people you are trying to attract.

3. Use your company page. This is a hidden gem. If you don't have one, make sure you create one, and more importantly, see Tip #2. Make sure that page excites the people you are trying to attract.

Des helps business owners use LinkedIn as a key platform to create new business and engage with clients. More at www.LeadGen2020.com/des.

---

[6] Testimonial from Mary Jo Manzanares, "Testimonials," *30 Day Linking Blitz*, accessed August 2013, http://30daylinkingblitz.com/testimonials/.

22

Content Drives Awareness

Content marketing strategies offer a way to generate awareness as well as nurturing leads of all sorts.

Content marketing is probably the most effective marketing tactic that exists today in the digital world. We can't hope to effectively address this tactic in just one rule; thus, we'll focus on the high points in this rule and offer you additional insight at www.LeadGen2020.com/content.

At its rawest, content marketing involves sharing content with the purpose of acquiring leads and converting them to customers. When it is all said and done, almost any company can use content marketing to some extent. This plays directly into a significant benefit of using LinkedIn, which is the ability to share and receive content, news, and relevant event invitations.

Be Thoughtful in the Way You Promote Your Own Content

In terms of content, people focus on things they value. Make sure that you are constantly interacting and engaging with your connections by sharing relevant company news and industry developments. A big bonus of content generation is bringing awareness to your brand. When people come to see your content, you will have the chance to show them the quality your brand offers. Your brand will have a positive association with rich quality content.

The more times you articulate value to your target audience, the more likely you are to find people who are interested in what you have to say. Be sure to strike a balance between engaging and encouraging engagement through your own content and content created by others. Ultimately, by being active and posting content, it enables you to stay top-of-mind and **position yourself as a helpful and trusted connection** in order to attract more business.

Content marketing strategies offer a way to generate awareness as well as nurturing leads of all sorts. Even when a lead has become a customer, rich content will continue to draw them back.

Building Out Your Content Plan for LinkedIn

1. **Do not be intimidated by the idea of "content."** Content can come in many different forms: videos, images, press releases, news, comments, and blogs. Anything that will entice your connections to interact and engage with you or your company will be of benefit.

2. **Set aside time.** Every month you need to set a time to plan the content you want to write for your website. Make it a regular date on the calendar, like the second Monday of the month.

3. **Consider your goals.** Perhaps you want to attract more endorsements on a certain skill or add connections from a certain industry, etc.

4. **Define the "value."** Remember, you are posting content to position yourself at the intersection of your client's interests or needs and your skills.

5. **Create a content schedule.** You may want to put out content every day, a couple of times a week, or once a week. Just make sure you space it out and keep it fresh.

6. **Find content.** There are numerous types of places to find content. You could use "LinkedIn Today" as that is always chock full of content. You can source content from your groups, from articles you are reading, from items you are writing, and many more ways too.

7. **Post content.** LinkedIn activity stream, groups, specific e-mails to your connections, and replies to people contacting you.

8. **Monitor the results.** Do some basic analysis. Check to see if you've moved toward the goals you've set out to achieve.

Next Steps

By now, we all understand that content is king. Creating and distributing interesting content is fundamental in generating awareness online, and what better place is there to circulate this content than an online network of professionals? By creating valuable content about your industry and distributing it via LinkedIn, you are establishing yourself and your business as thought leaders among a network of other professionals.

23 Content Marketing— Making the Intangible Tangible

Jay Deragon's Success

What is success on LinkedIn? Throughout this book, there are a variety of definitions from people that have achieved all kinds of results. We would like to introduce you to another one from Jay Deragon (www.Relationship-Economy.com). Jay is a prolific writer but not a professional journalist. He has strategically embraced the power of content marketing. As such, he hasn't paid a penny for any kind of marketing or advertising in over five years and has been able to drive the growth of his numerous businesses through LinkedIn. Yet he doesn't define LinkedIn success by the "traditional bottom line." For Jay, success on LinkedIn is a result of understanding the "ecosystem of your brand" and effectively pursuing the process to grow it.

Content as a Currency

One concept of content marketing that many people struggle with is that, at its core, content marketing is intangible. Yet people struggle to try and convert it directly to some sort of tangible return.

Jay shared a very unique perspective of content marketing with us. He described an ecosystem of relationships that are attracted by both content in your profile and the content you share from your profile. This creates a "currency," which is called a "relationship," and that is what he noted LinkedIn is all about.

Jay views LinkedIn and all its related tools as a platform for the trading of this conversational currency. This currency is traded in the form of content you share. A conversation turns to currency when people discover something meaningful within the conversation and they spread it as if it were their own. Conversations about brand experiences, topical perspectives, and innovative ideas have become the new currency that reflects the worth of our individual brands.

Now think about this. Conversations propagate based on the rate of interest. The value of your content is based on the rate of change of your updates, that is, how many times it changes hands. Rate of interest in your conversation is reflected by the rate of change. The more your conversation "changes" from one to one, to one to a million, the higher the interest rate becomes. Jay summed this up with an analogy on bankers—they don't care about money per se; they care about the rate of change of money.

Precision to Cut through the Noise and Engage Directly with Those Seeking His Value

Bolstered by this strategy, Jay posts five days a week. Each morning, he starts the day by adding a post and then posting this throughout the 50 groups he participates in. He posts items of value to groups he continually vets. In many ways, this is akin to fishing. He supplies valuable information, and then when people engage it, he can focus directly on communicating with those people. No day is complete without spending time in LinkedIn Today, reading what key thought leaders are sharing. This in turn could be material for future posts to share with his six thousand plus contacts that grow each day.

Jay's Tips

1. Focus on your desired result. If you don't have one, define it now.

2. Take a good hard look at your profile. There are always going to be items to change. Maximize your profile and leverage the "rate of change" to increase your awareness.

3. Make use of LinkedIn Today. It is filled with tremendous insight and thought leaders. Three quick benefits: learning, exhibiting your value, and engaging with others.

4. There is a wealth of info on LinkedIn. Take the time to study it and generate more insight about your prospects, employees, and competition.

Jay is a serial entrepreneur; member of AdAge Power 150; ranked Top 50 over 50 by Global CMO; an author; public speaker; and a proud dad, grandfather, and husband. Learn more at www.LeadGen2020/jay.

24 Learning How a LinkedIn "Like" Can Generate a Lead

People like recognition.

LinkedIn functions in a very similar way to the old "six degrees of Kevin Bacon" game, in which any actor can be linked through their film role to Kevin Bacon. In LinkedIn, connectivity can be a great conduit for awareness. Given the unique functionalities that LinkedIn provides, is it possible to turn a LinkedIn "like" into a lead?

What Is a "Like"?

Facebook has made the "like" function a natural part of browsing. It is a way to share information while passively communicating with a person at the same time. Now this concept is a functioning element on LinkedIn as well. First things first—a "like" creates recognition, which people welcome, especially those you have an existing relationship with. Have you ever posted something and nothing happened? No comments, no actions, no responses? We certainly have done this many times. How do you feel when someone clicks the "like" button under one of your posts? It is a feeling somewhere between reassurance and elation, knowing that people are watching and appreciating what you are doing.

The Impact of a "Like"

This section of the book is focused on generating awareness. Let's begin to explore how we might be able to use the option of hitting the "like" button to create a doorway to creating awareness and possibly a new lead. Hitting the "like" function may only **take a split second, but the impact can be much more significant.**

Consider the following:

- **People like recognition.** People like to have others pay attention to them and their accomplishments. When you "like" someone's profile or update, you are giving them that recognition. This provides an opening to further the conversation and grow your relationship with them.

- **A "like" helps keep your company in mind.** When you "like" something on LinkedIn, you keep your name in front of the person who made the post. In addition, your "like" shows up on your activity stream, which keeps you in front of all of your connections.

- **A "like" can be a great introduction.** If you "like" a company or one of its members, it offers a chance to make an introduction. It brings your name and company to the attention of someone in power. All of these can offer you entry to the right people in a company with which you want to do business.

- **It offers a chance for a quick hello.** Let's face it, we all want to keep in touch and relationship-build with our contacts, but there just isn't enough time in the day. A "like" is a quick way to let someone know you are thinking of them.

- **It offers another opportunity to share value to your network.** Since a "like" appears on the activity stream of your connections, if you found something interesting as it relates to your brand, it is going to be shared with your contacts too.

- **It offers another opportunity to comment.** In addition to hitting a "like," you are also able to add your insight in a comment section below, which offers another way for you to engage with that person and possibly your network too.

A "like" can be a very powerful (and simple) way to generate awareness. It is a stretch to think one "like" can directly turn into a lead, but it is well within the realm of possibility or even probability for a "like" to help you build the relationship that grows into trust. Who do people tend to do business with? Those they trust. Consider this function, and begin to leverage it as a tactic to help you increase your success on LinkedIn.

25 Generate Awareness by Making It Easy to Be Found

Any platform a business participates on in the social world should be optimized for search.

SEO, or search engine optimization, isn't just a buzzword for search engines and website developers anymore. In today's competitive world, SEO is an essential part of digital marketing and is getting noticed by potential prospects. Businesses are rapidly learning that effective SEO goes well beyond Google, Bing, or Yahoo!. Any platform a business participates on in the social world should be optimized for search, and this includes LinkedIn.

SEO: The Big Picture

Let's flip the perspective for SEO around for a moment. Think about SEO on LinkedIn like this. There are millions of users on the platform. If you were to perform a search, what criteria should LinkedIn use to provide you the most effective response to your search request? Clearly, LinkedIn is going to want to find the best attributes to tie back to the search query. What do they have to work with? Actually, quite a lot—everything from your profile to your participation. While their algorithm is not publicly known, based on general search parameters, we can highlight some things you should consider addressing in your use of LinkedIn.

- **Complete your profile.** Fill in the elements LinkedIn recommends (see Rule #14). LinkedIn probably wouldn't emphasize these if they weren't relevant.

- **Brainstorm keywords to include in your profile.** If a set of words is not in your profile, you will not come up in the search results when someone types them in. Think of all of the words, products, and concepts a potential client may use that relate to you. Check out other similar profiles to yours, and see words they use. Do searches of keywords you think might fit, and see who comes up at the top of the searches. Review their profiles, and make a specific note to see how keywords were used. Ultimately, build a list of the most effective keywords for you, and put them in your profile.

- **Optimize keywords in your job titles and descriptions (both past and present).** Don't be shy about what you did and the impact your role had on the organization. Stay away from generic job titles. Use words that reflect action and the true scope of the position. If you had a specialty, include it right in the title. Try to include keywords in your job titles in a way that is true to the actual position but leverages the SEO influence that LinkedIn has. Stay away from a list of skills that are purely a list of keywords.

- **Get creative with anchor text.** For instance, under "contact information," use a descriptive term that reflects you and your value compared to accepting the standard "my website" title.

A Note of Caution

In general, SEO is effective when used with informational text that has meaning. Text that is an obvious use of keywords, without any true "meat" to it, can work to your detriment. SEO may help someone find you, but using keywords just for keywords sake can quickly minimize the value you are trying to exude on LinkedIn.

Also, be cognizant that LinkedIn is being searched by the search engines as well. Things you say and post on the site can potentially be pulled up outside of LinkedIn. Perhaps the best thing to do is use this simple rule of thumb: if you wouldn't be comfortable stating something or making a specific comment at a networking event, don't post it on LinkedIn.

Your Benefit

SEO takes some strategic thought and effort but can be a powerful tool to generate awareness with people seeking your expertise. It's free. It can get you in front of those looking for you. It doesn't disappear overnight, and when done correctly, it also strongly supports your brand.

26 Effective Awareness through Invites

Invitations can be a unique differentiator.

LinkedIn invitations are a very simple and easy way to generate awareness to your profile. First off, it connects you with someone. Thus, they are aware of you being on LinkedIn. Secondly, and more importantly, it opens up the opportunity for you to continue to passively communicate with your contacts through your updates.

Let's begin with the basics. Each registered user has a number of "connections" on LinkedIn. Thus, if you have 55 connections, you have 55 people whom you've either invited to be part of your network or vice versa. Keeping with the basics for a moment longer, for two people to "connect," one must invite the other, and the other must accept. Pretty simple.

Now let's focus on increasing the effectiveness of the invite as a tactic for generating awareness.

Effort is more than just hitting the "accept" or "send" buttons. We are talking about generating awareness, and awareness takes a little bit of effort. Plan to spend at least a couple of moments on every invitation you send or receive.

Avoid using the invitation default. One of the most common things to do on LinkedIn is to send an invite with a default invitation stating, "I would like to connect with you on LinkedIn." Yet as you read through our stories of success, you are going to notice, time and time again, that each of these people avoids the default invite and personalizes it to the person they are inviting. (Note: when using certain mobile tools for invitations, you are currently unable to do anything but send a default invite. Hopefully this changes in future app updates.)

Here is a general example highlighting the point above: *"Hi Chris, Enjoyed meeting you yesterday. There are a couple of people in my network that I think might be of benefit to you. I look forward to reviewing that with you when you have a free moment. Thanks, John."*

Respond to invitations. Admittedly, when someone sends you a default invite and you aren't sure why they've connected, it is hard to do anything more than accept the invite. Your LinkedIn network is only as valuable as the strength of your connections. Try to engage each invite you receive with a short note. The goal is twofold. First, try to determine if this is someone that fits with the audience you are trying to build, and second, it is a differentiator to leverage in relationship building.

Find people to invite. The most basic way for people to build their network is to start with their personal contact lists. People in these lists might include someone you have worked with, collaborated on projects with, or maybe attended school with. If you are so inclined, LinkedIn offers you the opportunity to upload your e-mails and have a mass invite. If this is something you are contemplating, consider balancing the urge for a mass invite with the benefits of a personalized invite.

Connect with care. A general rule of thumb is to send connection requests only to people you have something in common with. LinkedIn makes this very simple by graphically showing you what you have in common with each user. If you focus on things you have in common, you'll realize that, in many ways, this feature eliminates the dreaded "cold call."

Find more people to meet. Join groups that are in your area of expertise and niche markets. You may already have their acquaintance through discussion groups. Check out their profiles, and find other points in common. Create as much common ground as you can with your target or niche markets and prospects in the invite. Extending your awareness opens up opportunities for lead generation.

27 Don't Overlook InMails because They Cost Money

LinkedIn claims they are 30 percent more effective than using regular e-mails.

LinkedIn offers tools (for purchase) to members that can accelerate their lead generation efforts. One of these is InMail. InMail is the premium e-mail messaging service available for LinkedIn's members. It differs from normal LinkedIn e-mail because it allows you to message people outside your professional network.

The InMail Value

Those who use LinkedIn have a high confidence level in anything they receive through InMail. Since senders pay for each InMail sent, they tend to choose the people they contact with care. Thus, those that receive these messages are more likely to open these e-mails and to respond to the sender. The cool thing here is **if you don't get a reply within seven days, you get the credit back to your account** where it can sit for up to 90 days. In effect, you get a refund.

Thinking in terms of cost, InMails aren't cheap. If you purchase them individually, they cost 10 dollars each. Looking at this in terms of ROI, perhaps they are a good bang for your buck as you tend to get a very good response from them. LinkedIn claims they are 30 percent more effective than using regular e-mails.

How to Use LinkedIn InMail Successfully

Always have a clear purpose in mind when putting together an InMail message. Ask yourself this: What do you want to achieve by sending this InMail? You need to know whom you want to connect with. Also, make sure you craft your message around that person's profile and how your business can help meet his or her company needs. Keep the content light and be yourself.

How Does It Work?

- **Buy credits.** InMail is not a free option. LinkedIn offers members the chance to buy credits toward InMail. A free membership can buy up to 10 credits per month at 10 dollars a shot. Paid memberships get a limited amount of free InMail messages each month. They can also buy up to 10 extra credits each month.

- **Choose your target.** You need to know whom you are sending the message to. Have a clear target in mind. Do not mindlessly send a message to a person who you have no clue about. At the very least, make sure the person you are targeting is the right type of decision-maker to help your efforts.

- **Write your message.** Craft your message. Keep your note brief and to the point. Be clear what you are communicating. You are attempting to connect. Ask a question to get that person to respond. It is a great way to get his or her attention.

- **Include contact information.** Always include the name of your company, your name, your title, and contact information. The message will give the person a link to your LinkedIn profile. Make sure the profile is complete before sending the first InMail.

The Next Steps

LinkedIn InMail has value for many businesses but not all. The only way to find out if yours is one is to give it a try. If you want to try InMail for your marketing, the next step from the LinkedIn side is to:

- Purchase some credits and use InMail a while.

- Subscribe to a LinkedIn monthly upgrade and try the free InMail.

Another option would be to activate OpenLink. This is a free option available to premium members which allows OpenLink members to communicate with each other for free.

Make sure you put your effort into using InMail effectively. Some people set up InMail as an entire marketing campaign. Decide what is best for your business. Maximize your approach for InMails by setting up a roadmap for results.

28

There Are Immediate Paid Ways to Generate Leads Too

Vince Gelormine's insight: as with any online marketing tool, there are benefits and challenges.

The majority of the rules in this book are focused on organic (free) methods for generating leads. This one though, is focused on paid lead generation. As we all know, Google pioneered pay-per-click (PPC) and has made billions from it. Almost every other site has tried to copy this model. LinkedIn Ads (LI Ads) is LinkedIn's version of PPC on its own site.

The second edition of this book is focused on generating results. Thus, on the topic of PPC results, one person who has used them very successfully is Vince Gelormine, CEO of WebPromote, Inc., an Internet marketing agency specializing in PPC. Vince is also the author of two books on Internet marketing. While he may come across as an unassuming guy, don't let that fool you. Vince has successfully used PPC methods to grow and cash out one of his businesses to the tune of a seven-figure payday.

LinkedIn Ads

Let's start with the basics. LinkedIn Ads consist of a headline of up to 25 characters, a description of up to 75 characters, an image, and a URL. When we caught up with Vince, he had just finished a LinkedIn Ad campaign focused on generating conversions for a live event. As with any online marketing tool, there are benefits and challenges. On the benefits side, LinkedIn Ads provides the potential to reach a different level of user that is not readily accessible on other platforms. It generates lower click volume than other platforms, but even though these yield fewer leads, the quality tends to be better.

One challenge noted was that most people use LinkedIn for very short periods of time and usually go there for a purpose. This makes noticing any ad less likely than on Google where people are searching specifically for something. Another challenge as of this writing—LinkedIn does not have a built-in method of tracking conversions outside of the site.

Addressing a Challenge

Tracking is critical for any paid campaign. Thus, Vince shared a couple of potential workarounds for tracking:

- **Third-party tracking tools.** Create a URL for the campaign, and then place the tracking code on the "thank you" page of your lead capture form or transaction page. One possible tool is Adwatcher.com.

- **Google Analytics (or other analytics tools/software).** When set up properly, you can track results using analytics software.

- **Dedicated landing page.** Create a landing page that receives traffic only from LinkedIn. Thus, tracking conversions from the campaign will be simple to measure. The one negative to this approach, however, is that it requires a dedicated landing page for each campaign that is run with LI Ads.

Vince had a significant amount of insight to share on this topic. To learn more about his PPC insights you can go to www.LeadGen2020.com/webpromote.

Vince's Tips

1. If you are looking to get started, keep an eye out for promotional coupons. Every so often 50 dollar coupons are available for users to test this platform.

2. Make sure your daily budget can support the clicks you want for that day. For example, if you set a budget of 10 dollars per day and your bid is three dollars per click, you may get three to four clicks before your ad goes offline. If that's not enough clicks, then you'll want to set your budget higher.

3. Choose CPC over CPM, and bid high for clicks (high end of recommended range, if not two to three times more, to ensure proper visibility of your ads). Review every couple of days, and modify ads if CTR gets below 0.025 percent.

4. Closely monitor your campaign, especially over the first one to two days. Check it every four hours or so, and adjust your budget or make ad changes as necessary.

Section V
Engage

There are numerous ways to create engagement on LinkedIn by using your time efficiently. The goal is simple—add value and build relationships. Don't contribute to the noise on social media; focus on sharing insights and communicate directly with your audience in ways that add value to them.

In this section, we address a variety of ways that LinkedIn offers you to engage and relationship-build in a time-effective manner.

Rule 29: Sustained Engagement Builds Relationships

Rule 30: Effective Effort Creates LinkedIn Success

Rule 31: Companies Have Unique Abilities to Engage Too

Rule 32: Endorsements—Engagement with a Click

Rule 33: Engagement through Group Participation

Rule 34: Growing a Large LinkedIn Group with a Challenging Demographic

Rule 35: LinkedIn Mobile Apps—Engagement on the Go

Rule 36: Engagement—10 Tactics That Take Less than 10 Minutes

Sustained Engagement Builds Relationships

LinkedIn makes it incredibly simple for users to create engagement across their site.

Many people struggle with the concept of engagement on LinkedIn. Perhaps Facebook is partially to blame for this. In a broad sense, since Facebook is a very social site, there exists a certain level of engagement between typical Facebook users and their connections before they connect. Hence, this is possibly why they are called "friends."

While you don't have "friends" on LinkedIn, you do have "connections." Perhaps this is mirrored after the business world. It is up to us to engage our business connections and build relationships with them. Thus, the third leg of our methodology focuses on ways to create and build engagement on LinkedIn.

Engagement builds relationships. Relationships build trust, and in business, whom do you tend to do business with? You tend to do business with people you trust.

Engagement Is Critical to Your Roadmap for Results

Good news here! LinkedIn makes it incredibly simple for users to create engagement across their site. Let's review some of the tools:

"**Old school.**" Back in the day, engagement used to occur across a "three-martini lunch." While it no longer exists, meeting someone face-to-face for lunch or coffee (i.e., today's version of the three-martini lunch) is a fantastic engagement tool. Review your

LinkedIn contacts, and set up a schedule to try and meet with those you are connected to.

Build out and participate from your LinkedIn company page. This is a fantastic way to engage directly in a multimedia way regarding your value and your business.

Endorsements. We are going to explore this more deeply in Rule #32, but as we've seen, people like recognition, and supplying someone an endorsement achieves this. At its most basic level, it takes literally a second to endorse someone.

Join a group. (See more in Rule #33.) This is a great way to show your value (no spamming or selling), and there is enormous engagement potential by being the person starting a topic. You have people reading something you wrote, and they are potentially writing back to you. Of course, you have the ability to write back to them. Communication starts, and relationships can start and grow.

"Sharing" button. The LinkedIn widget is now attached to most articles that show up on the web. In less than 10 seconds after you click the button, you can share the information with (a) your activity stream, (b) on Twitter, (c) various groups you are in, and (d) specific people within your network. Again, focus on the value you can share; don't spam or brag.

Messaging. As noted in the point above, you can share articles directly to people in your network. What about sending them a quick note to say hello? It still works in terms of relationship-building, and in a world of simply hitting a button to engage, a simple, short note is a big differentiator.

Commenting. Whether you are at a desktop or on the LinkedIn app, you can share your thoughts about something that has been posted by someone in your network or groups. This is another simple point of communication.

Opposite of Engagement

While we are on the topic of engagement, let's address the opposite of this for a moment. This is a question we frequently hear: How do I remove a connection? Sometimes, there may be people who you no longer want to be part of your network. Removing a connection from your list is actually a pretty simple function. There are multiple ways to do that. An easy one is to go to their profile; right near their photo you will see a bar to "suggest connections." Click on that, and at the bottom of it, you can remove this connection. If you do remove a connection, the removal is neither captured in any alert nor is the other member notified.

30 Effective Effort Creates LinkedIn Success

Lorraine Ball's Success: generate results by understanding the difference between activity and productivity.

LinkedIn success. Millions of people talk about it, but how many have actually achieved it? It really does happen! The important thing to keep in mind is that when it happens, you typically see someone following a productive, focused path versus someone simply haphazardly participating on LinkedIn.

A great example of this is seen through following Lorraine Ball, or the "whirlwind" as she is affectionately known in her business www.RoundPeg.biz. She leads a team of "crazy, passionate" people that help small businesses become big businesses with simple, cost-effective marketing strategies.

Simply spend two minutes talking with Lorraine, and it will become very obvious why she has successfully leveraged LinkedIn to generate a series of successes for her business. The secret? She doesn't focus on herself. She is genuine in her interest of engaging the people she is communicating with in terms of sharing items that provide them value. She is never "selling" anything to anybody. Make no mistake, she doesn't like being sold to either. You spam, boast, or advertise your way into her inbox, and you take the risk of being her ex-LinkedIn connection.

A 140-Character Update Leads to Ongoing Revenue from All over the United States

Serendipity and strategy usually work hand in hand to generate success on LinkedIn. Perhaps a quote from Oprah Winfrey states it best: "Luck is simply preparation meeting opportunity."[7] The seeds for most success on LinkedIn can start simply but only in the context of an effective strategy.

Lorraine's successes on LinkedIn exhibit this well. Throughout a typical day, she provides three status updates that flow into her activity stream seen by all of her connections. She also checks in with the groups she participates with. At one time, like many other LinkedIn users, she was a member in numerous groups but that was very inefficient. Now to increase the effectiveness of her group participation, she only focuses on three groups in which she can add the most value.

While a daily update is a fairly simple and common thing, Lorraine ensures that her updates offer elements of significance to her connections, and this is what led to one of her biggest LinkedIn successes.

As is Lorraine's habit, she checks LinkedIn first thing in the morning and provides her first update. A former coworker she was connected to saw her update and invited her to speak at an upcoming sales meeting. Lorraine accepted and presented to a sales group that included over one hundred distributors from all over the United States. Based on that talk, some of the sales leaders in the audience approached her to hire her to present to their home districts. Three years and thousands of dollars later, the phone is still ringing, and Lorraine is still receiving revenue, generating work that stemmed from that one particular update.

Lorraine's Tips

1. Connect, connect, connect. The more connections you have, the more potential people you can relationship-build with. Reach out to former bosses, coworkers, colleagues, and friends. Reestablish and nurture these relationships. Whom do people tend to do business with? Those they trust and have relationships with.

2. Avoid the auto-feed tools. Yes, it saves time, but it tends to eliminate the ability to effectively engage connections, which in turn severely limits your LinkedIn success.

3. Don't contribute to the noise on social media. Focus on sharing insights and communicate directly with your audience in ways that add value to them. Share tips, insights, best practices, "likes," etc., that your audience can benefit from.

Lorraine helps business owners incorporate LinkedIn into a comprehensive online strategy. Learn more at www.LeadGen2020.com/roundpeg.

---

[7] Oprah, "Be Prepared – Oprah – Quotes on Luck – Oprah.com," Oprah.com, accessed August 2013, http://www.oprah.com/spirit/Thought-for-Today-Luck.

31 Companies Have Unique Abilities to Engage Too

The hidden gem in LinkedIn marketing.

Perhaps one of the hidden "gems" that currently exists in generating results in LinkedIn is the "company page." Your company page provides an introduction to your company, the brand, and the people behind both. Think of it as a combination business card, brochure, and store window. It offers a portal into your company so potential leads can get a glimpse of what you have to offer at the business and human level.

Just the Highlights

- From a marketing perspective, some of the things you can use your company page for include generating leads, attracting new talent, and engaging your target audience.
- Functionally, your company page can do a few things your personal profile can't, like targeted updates and update stats.
- People can follow your company page without having to connect with you personally.

Quick Tips to Start

Create Your Company Welcome

- Provide imagery. You can use an image that showcases your value or brand and welcomes your visitors.
- Give an introduction to the company and how it started.
- Offer a brief bio on your key people. Try to personalize and show the human side of them.

Engage Your Audience

- Converse with your target audience via status

updates. (Note: your company page updates will be completely separate from your personal profile updates.)

- Offer an introduction to your products and services. This does not mean putting them all in a long bullet point list. It means creating a meaningful article that details what you have to offer.
- Leverage targeted updates. A company can choose whether to send in its status update to all followers or a more focused audience, which it can select based on industry, company size, geography, seniority, or function.

Generate Buzz

- Ask current customers for testimonials and recommendations. Highlight this on your company page.
- Offer interesting content that people will want to share with others. This will bring more people to the page.
- Keep visitors engaged and talking by making your LinkedIn presence count. Become a part of discussion groups, create interesting content, and offer multimedia presentations. All of these will get people engaged for the long term.

Get to Know Your Audience

- Behind the scenes, you can use analytics to understand who your followers are. These will give you insight on how well your LinkedIn presence is doing and may give you direction on where to take it.
- Who is most often visiting your company page? You may see some visitors coming more than once and a few only once.
- What industries are they from? Ideally, you will see people from the industries you want to target coming to see what you have to offer

Quick Examples of Interesting Sales Pages

- Hubspot[8] (marketing company): they are using company pages as a lead gen tool. They populate their products page with links for free reports, which captures new leads.
- Dell (large company): they have very strong use of rich media, graphics, and videos to support and highlight their user engagement and talent acquisition. As of this writing, they have just under a half million followers.
- Tata Consultancy Services (international company): they have a well-designed page, integrating the use of video, and they have a few hundred thousand company followers.
- The IT Media Group (small company): they were selected by LinkedIn as having one of the best company pages in 2012.[9]

---

[8] For purposes of transparency, as of this writing, Chris is a Hubspot-certified partner. You can contact him at www.linkedin.com/in/ChrisMuccio to learn more.

[9] Lana Khavinson, "Announcing The 12 Best LinkedIn Company Pages of 2012 [SLIDESHOW]," *LinkedIn* (blog), December 12, 2012, http://blog.linkedin.com/2012/12/12/best-linkedin-company-pages-of-2012/.

Endorsements—
Engagement with a Click

Time has a value too. Don't overlook the effort-to-reward ratio of an endorsement.

Why does a virtual pat on the back create such passionate opposing views? Perhaps the answer has to do with the way people view the meaning of the endorsement function. Some people find endorsements absolutely worthless, while others love them. Our goal is not to debate the merits or detriments of these but to show how they can be used for **engagement**.

Why Is an Endorsement Valuable?

Let's start by addressing the big elephant in the room. Do people currently base their decision on what a person's value is based on the number of endorsements they have? Given the passions aroused by this function, clearly some are. However, when we put this question to an audience of about one hundred people and asked them to raise their hand if they based decisions on the number of endorsements, **not one** person's hand went up. Clearly, not a scientific sample, but certainly one that has anecdotal insight.

So if the value of an endorsement is not to have others base their beliefs of your value on it, then where's the benefit?

At its most basic level, it takes literally a second to click an endorsement. It is a quick way to endorse someone you know and make them feel good about it. Thus, it is a very simple way to engage with someone. This in turn can become a conversation starter. For instance, many people that receive an endorsement will turn around and send a quick message of thanks to the person sending it. This can lead to increased communication and interaction, which are exactly what are needed to grow trust.

Years back when we wrote the first edition, LinkedIn based part of its search algorithm on a user inputting "specialties" into their profile. Specialties have evolved into "skills," and skills are the basis for endorsements. Thus, logic would dictate that endorsements factor into LinkedIn's algorithm for keyword search.

Time Has a Value Too

Don't overlook the effort-to-reward ratio of an endorsement. We want to be active on LinkedIn. We want to add value and relationship-build on LinkedIn, but we don't have unlimited time to do this. Given the time invested in endorsement versus the good will, the engagement, the "SEO-oomph", as well as showing up on your connection's activity streams, the reward is very significant!

A Couple of Things to Keep in Mind

We want to be sensitive to the people that are not believers in endorsements. Please keep in mind that only first-level connections can endorse another person, so the assumption is you should already know the person (and we understand that we should never assume). Also, it is up to you as to whether you want to accept the endorsements. You may reject the ones in which you feel are not right.

We do not make it a practice to endorse people we don't know or their skills we aren't aware of. It is clear that others do, but ultimately, it is up to you as to how you want to progress with this function.

One last thing to keep in mind, with over one billion made already, endorsements are not going away any time soon. If this "recommendation lite" function bothers you, then follow a set of guidelines you can live with, but please do not ignore endorsements. As of now, their use and benefits are just scratching the surface. Stay ahead of the curve as this feature develops, and always consider your business focus as the guide for your roadmap to results.

33 Engagement through Group Participation

Offer awesome solutions and insight through your group participation.

Participating in LinkedIn groups can be a very effective tool in your roadmap for results if you know how to find the right groups, effectively contribute, and sustain that over time. At its core, a group should be a central place to host discussions with people, particularly those with the same interests as you. Members should be engaged, value should be shared, and relationships should be grown.

Join Many Groups, Participate in a Few, Manage One

Currently, LinkedIn allows its members to join up to 50 groups, and of course, everyone is free to start and grow their own group. There is complete freedom to join groups regardless of their classification. However, if you want to join a "closed" group, you will have to meet certain criteria that the group manager has created. Once in a group, the key is to be an active participant that adds value in the group.

As we've learned since the beginning of this book, the goal is to keep your LinkedIn participation aligned with your business focus. Applying this to LinkedIn groups, it means finding the right ones to match your business goals. We suggest you find five that you can focus on participating in.

Finding Five Groups That Fit Your Roadmap for Results

Perhaps the easiest way to start would be to:

- Check the profiles of your current LinkedIn connections that you value and see their list of

LinkedIn groups. Again, concentrate on groups that align with your business focus.

- Join up to five groups, and then vet them once you've become a member. What you are specifically looking for is (a) the amount of participation in the group, (b) the amount of engagement within the group, and (c) the "value" that is being shared. If you see self-promotions and self-advertising, these are red flags.

An additional way to find groups is through the search function. When searching groups, LinkedIn tells searchers how "active" the groups are and displays the number of discussions started in those groups in the most recent month. Low activity doesn't necessarily preclude success. Keep in mind that many people are somewhat timid to participate but they do "lurk" and read the posts. Thus, if your target audience hangs out here and if you take an active role (e.g., always offering value, solutions, etc.), you can still be very effective in creating awareness and engagement. The suggestion here would be to join an "active" group with the number of discussions that suit you.

If you find you've joined a group that doesn't offer you the value you are seeking, remember, you can always leave a group and find another to join. The suggestion here might be to follow this path until you have found five groups that you can genuinely participate in and have them be an effective relationship building tool.

Being Active

Your goal is to be active in your five main groups. People want to see that you are active, that you give back, and that you know what you are talking about. Groups allow members to post articles, start conversations, reply to existing threads, and post "likes."

Participate in the conversation, ask questions, and answer other people's questions earnestly. If you have content, share it, but be sure it is relevant to the topic. The more you contribute to your group and the more you give and share content, the more value members place on you.

Ultimately, when you offer awesome solutions and insight into client issues in groups, group members will click on your name to check out your profile and learn more about you.

Joining Our Group

If you would like to join our group, please go to www.LeadGen2020.com/linkedin. This will take you to our LinkedIn group.

34
Growing a Large LinkedIn Group with a Challenging Demographic

Cindy Kraft's Success

In today's digital age, CFOs are an enigma. Chris has spent a significant part of his career working on that side of the organization so he's always tried to evolve with the changing times and thought others have as well. The current reality is most CFOs have yet to fully embrace how the evolving digital landscape impacts them. This is very clearly seen on LinkedIn where there are thousands upon thousands of people who use the term "CFO" in their titles yet display almost nothing that highlights this "distinction" in their profiles or in their LinkedIn communications.

The business need is clear: help CFOs and senior finance executives maximize their marketability and overall ability to compete in today's digital age. Ready to meet this need is Cindy Kraft, the "CFO-Coach." A few years back while working as a generalist, Cindy made a decision that would be tough for many small business owners to make. This was her decision "to transition from a generalist to a subject matter expert" working exclusively with very senior finance executives. Clearly, while that reduced the playing field, it solidified her positioning and significantly raised her visibility in that smaller space.

Looking back, the risky decision to focus solely on the financial executive niche has turned out very well. While it did take her almost two years of persistence, she is now clearly recognizable as the subject matter expert in this space. When people search for a CFO coach, her name is the first one that pops up.

LinkedIn Success: Growing a Large Group While Keeping Pure to Her Focus

Cindy has been razor sharp on her focus. Her success on LinkedIn stems from the CFO group she has built from the ground up. As with everything she does, this is highly specific. The group is only for CFOs. It is a closed group, meaning you can't simply join and automatically become part of the group. Actually, you need to pass the minimum requirement of currently holding the CFO title or having held the CFO title in the recent past and exhibit the value a typical CFO should have on LinkedIn. If your profile doesn't exude that value, you won't be admitted into this group. While she accepts personal connections with headhunters, they are not allowed to participate in this group. This is a group built purely and simply just for financial executives.

Cindy spends the majority of her time on LinkedIn, focused on her group. She is perpetually sharing insights of value to CFOs on topics related to their careers. Her group receives tremendous value from Cindy, and in turn, she has a completely filtered target audience with whom to communicate.

When Cindy started the group, she thought she would be happy to one day have a couple of hundred group members. Instead, she currently has over 1,200! Interestingly, as this group grows, logic would seem to suggest that participation among the group members would grow proportionately. Yet, this is still evolving. Cindy noted many executives don't yet realize that social media is a two-way communication. They are still "stuck" in the old style type of one-way media. Ultimately, this issue ties to her goal as evangelizing the importance of LinkedIn and getting her audience to really understand the value of becoming more visible on the site as it is critically important to their market value.

Cindy's Tips

1. Your headline is not your job title.

2. If you don't have a compelling summary, they probably won't read any further.

3. Your profile must be consistently maintained.

America's leading career and personal brand strategist for corporate finance executives: Cindy@CFO-Coach.com, 813-655-0658, or www.LeadGen2020.com/cfo-coach.

35 LinkedIn Mobile Apps— Engagement on the Go

Expect frequent updates that offer a nice supplement to your desktop usage.

In any strategic business discussion today, the topic of mobile needs to be included. LinkedIn recently unveiled revamped versions of its iPhone, Android, and web apps to focus heavily on content and personalization. The challenge with writing about these new apps is that we live in a world where mobile apps are being updated fairly frequently. Thus, something we write about here is almost certain to be updated within the next couple of months. Make sure to double-check that the functionality we are writing about still works as described.

As of this writing, LinkedIn mobile usage is growing and now accounts for 27 percent of its unique visitors. Interestingly, the company found that mobile users aren't browsing the social network in the same way as desktop users. The newly designed apps address these differences and put a new visual activity stream, full of stories and status updates, front and center. In previous versions of their mobile app, the idea behind the stream was to present members with small, mobile-appropriate bits of information. Now, the focus is on helping people easily take actions.

Engagement

If you have an iPhone, one thing we've made a lot of use of is the ability to refer to your connections on the go. For instance, if you click on your connections on your main screen or if you search for a particular contact, you can ultimately see that person's profile.

Say you just left a meeting with him or her. You can e-mail that person directly from LinkedIn—nothing like immediate feedback to help you make a positive impression. We often use this tool prior to a meeting. By getting refreshed on what the person is working on, what they may have recently posted, or just reviewing who you are connected to in common can help create a positive impression. All of these are accessible from the palm of your hand. Lastly, ever forget a phone number? If someone has entered their phone number in the "contact" section of their profile, you have access to it as well.

Invitations

This differs from the iPad to the iPhone to the Android. One very inefficient thing is the inability to personalize an invitation to someone. On the iPhone, you can invite someone and get a message that pops up which can be lightly customized. That at least is a good thing. With the iPad and the Android, currently all you can do is send the default invitation when you want to connect with someone. Our hope is LinkedIn will adjust this at some point, as this is a very important element to use in your relationship-building. A very simple workaround for now is to invite the person from your desktop.

Endorsements

One commonality across all mobile apps currently available is the inability to endorse colleagues (which currently is reserved only for visitors to LinkedIn's main site). While the endorsement feature is not the most used feature of LinkedIn, it is effective in solidifying a new relationship. An example of this can be evidenced when attending trade shows. Where the mobile app provides you with the opportunity to add a new contact while on site, you're unable to endorse the new contact, acknowledging an aspect of your conversation that you found significant, until you're back at the office.

Today

Mobile apps give users more of a reason to look at LinkedIn while on the go. While the current versions are still a couple of elements away from providing all the results-building tools you need on the go, they still offer significant power away from the office. Stay tuned, keep plugged in, and be attentive to the updates that are being released, specifically understanding how each one impacts the mobile benefit you receive.

36

Engagement—10 Tactics That Take Less than 10 Minutes

The goal is to help you create a sustainable participation on LinkedIn.

There are numerous ways to create engagement on LinkedIn by using your time efficiently. If you are building out a 15-minute-per-day participation plan, these tactics should fit perfectly. In this rule, we are going to discuss 10 tactics that can each be performed in well under 10 minutes. (Note: these are all online techniques. You could always integrate offline techniques like writing a note and mailing it and sending a card.)

Quickest Tactics: Each Takes Less than a Couple of Minutes

1. Start your day with a quick glance at your notifications tab (located, as of this writing, at the top right of your page). In a couple of seconds, you can see who has most recently interacted with you. Based on that, you can respond accordingly.

2. Check your morning e-mails with group activity. Scan to see which posts you are interested in and can comment effectively toward.

3. Open up your Google Alerts, and scan for interesting information to share with your connections. (Note: if you haven't already, set up Google Alerts to monitor keyword phrases that are important to you, your industry, or your target audience. Each day, Google sends you an e-mail with a list of articles related to your search. It takes less than a minute to initially set up.) Always add a sentence or two to the link you post. Just posting links without

comments does not create the engagement you want people to make with you. One note of caution: be cognizant of articles that you come across that may be sitting behind a site's paid side (i.e., paywall). Some recipients won't be able to read these links.

4. Scan your activity stream. Depending on how you have your filter set, this can show all the activity occurring within your network. Find items to comment on in a value-added way. Making relevant comments keeps you and your company name in people's thoughts and reinforces the connections between you. If you can't find something to comment on, then find something to "like." As we discussed in Rule #24, it can still be a powerful tactic.

5. Endorse someone in your network. Consider the points we shared in Rule #32.

Quick Tactics: Each Takes Less than Five Minutes

6. When people endorse you, thank them. If they commented on your update, respond. If they viewed your profile, send them a message.

7. Skip the e-mail in item #2, and go directly into your key groups. Open each one and post a comment, comment on a post, or add a "like." Always add value to the discussion. Just do this in your main groups. Spreading yourself too thin will dilute your effectiveness.

8. Post an update on your company page. It is a great way to engage with a highly targeted demographic.

9. Focus on one-to-one communication. Check out specific profiles in your network. You can see the last time you've communicated with them via LinkedIn's little CRM function. Take a quick second to send a short message.

10. Invite people. Take a few minutes to find new people to add to your network. They may be people in your target industry, region, or company. Make a connection request with a personal message. Perform this wisely. Remember to connect with care and with those you have something in common with. Don't spam invites; LinkedIn is watching.

Next Steps

Take a look at these tactics. Try them. Refine them and figure out what works best for you. The goal is to help you create a sustainable participation on LinkedIn. These are quick and can be very effective tools to engage with your target audiences.

Section VI
Convert

As we've shared throughout this book, the path to generating results starts with "strategy," followed by "awareness generation," which then requires "engagement." Successfully working these elements together puts you on your way to your desired "conversion." Interestingly, a conversion is a relative term. It doesn't mean the same thing to each person. Thus, we've shared a variety of success stories for you to read about what others are doing to generate their success on LinkedIn.

Rule 37: Conversion—Putting All the Pieces Together

Rule 38: Digital Insight Increases the Ability to "Make It Rain"

Rule 39: It's Not about Selling—You Have to Educate and Provide Great Information

Rule 40: Podcasting + LinkedIn Generates Conversions

Rule 41: 11 Clients from LinkedIn before Having a Website

Rule 42: Generating Your Conversions

37

Conversion—Putting All the Pieces Together

Antoine Dupont's Success

Throughout this book, we've broken down elements of our methodology and presented them to you as individual rules. As we focus on "conversions," we thought it would be interesting to see an example of all of these elements working together with LinkedIn as an integral part of this process. This is a somewhat "live" example as this process was only started a few months back and is currently in motion as of this writing.

Generating a Conversion Is a Lot Like Dating

The funny thing about the lead gen process is that it is very similar to dating. For instance, let's say you've just generated interest from someone new on LinkedIn. Does that person know you well or is that person immediately ready to make a purchase from you? Most likely, the answer is no, and this is very similar to a "first date." You and the other person need to focus on getting to know each other better before you can expect to move the relationship along.

In a lead gen context, this is known as "lead nurturing," which is a continued communication with a prospect to help build up his or her interest in doing business with you. We want to introduce you to Antoine Dupont, CEO of Admin eSolutions. Antoine has been growing his business through generating leads via social media channels and then nurturing them through his conversion process. Antoine participates across all of the main social sites, but through this campaign, LinkedIn is driving 10 times the amount of leads back to his website when compared to all of the other social media combined!

LinkedIn Success Is Driving Traffic to Your Website from Your Target Audience

Antoine's target audiences are small-business owners that are dissatisfied with their current web/Internet solutions. His strategy to communicate is simple. It is all about posting the value this audience is interested in. These include checklists, tips, and how-to stories.

To kick off their lead gen process, they've created several prospect personas that helped them determine where they could find their target audience on LinkedIn. Once found, Antoine uses existing tools within LinkedIn to monitor and participate in relevant conversations throughout the business week. They've experimented with interacting during weekends but found much more traffic was derived during the work week.

Driving Traffic, Creating a Lead, and Nurturing That into a Sale

Admin eSolution's lead gen process starts with traffic generation from a variety of channels. In terms of traffic from their social media channels, LinkedIn drives 88 percent of it. Viewers arrive at Antoine's site because they are interested in reading more about something he posted on LinkedIn. Once the person arrives on their site, the goal is to generate a lead, which Antoine defines as anyone who requests more information or downloads a white paper, guide, or eBook he offers.

Using their prospecting personas again, Antoine's team investigates each lead. They look at each profile, current business, current website, and geo location, and determine whether they've gained a "qualified" lead or not.

Once they have a qualified lead, they use an industry-leading marketing tool to funnel qualified leads directly to a series of specifically timed e-mails. Each e-mail contains "value-based" content. This content is targeted to a specific audience. Then Antoine monitors who is actually reading/clicking the e-mails (a.k.a. who is engaged). When they are engaged (a.k.a. a hot lead), they use a more direct approach such as a personal e-mail and a phone call. Currently, Antoine's team is focusing on lead-nurturing 31 qualified leads that were generated directly from LinkedIn.

Antoine's Tip

Be engaged, be helpful, and be consistent. Nobody wants to hear about your products or services. They are looking for something to resolve their issues/pain.

Antoine helps small-business owners to position their website and Internet strategy from an expense to a lead-generating tool. Learn more at www.LeadGen2020.com/adminesolutions.

38 Digital Insight Increases the Ability to "Make It Rain"

Chad Van Horne's Success

Can LinkedIn generate success for the millennial generation today, or do they have to "pay their dues" first? Theoretically, LinkedIn should be a more powerful tool for people as they become more senior in their career. They have more experiences and can demonstrate this through their achievements. Well, this is not a maxim, and to prove this, we would like to introduce you to someone who has achieved significant success on LinkedIn before he has reached his 30th birthday.

What Can a Digital Rainmaker Accomplish?

How many people do you know under 30 that have met the president of the United States? We would like to introduce you to one: Chad Van Horn, a law firm partner. Meeting a president and becoming a partner at a law firm are bucket list items for many people, but not for Chad. They are simply an extension of something he does very well. He knows how to effectively use digital tools to "make it rain."

Forget his age; Chad's success is rooted in his business philosophy. He strongly believes that you should "give before you get" but do it in a way that is mutually beneficial. For instance, he likes to routinely give free advice, as it is a way to demonstrate one's knowledge without bragging. He is also quick to provide a recommendation or endorsement for someone in his network. They tend to return the favor, both online and offline, in terms of recommending clients.

In addition, he has received many endorsements for his understanding of bankruptcy, which is his concentration. To build upon this, whenever he receives a new endorsement, he sends a message and thanks the person for endorsing him. It's another way to continue to relationship-build.

Chad's ability to enact his philosophy effectively in a digital world created a very unique opportunity for him. Becoming a partner in a law firm is not something most lawyers are considered for unless they have 15 or 20 years of experience under their belt. However, social media, and LinkedIn specifically, changed that for Chad.

Chad shared how this success came about for him. He noted that the firm pursuing him was focused on finding good potential partners who had strong social media marketing, and the first place they looked was LinkedIn. Given the millions of people on LinkedIn, Chad stood out because he had a very coordinated digital marketing profile, with LinkedIn literally being his "quarterback" for it all.

Sounds simple, but it wasn't. In the legal world, reputation is critical. It is the number one advertising element attorneys have. One of the basic tenets of an attorney is their attorney-client privilege. While that is formally "protected," client trust is earned, not legally sanctioned. Thus, an attorney who wants to compete in the digital era needs to understand how to effectively express that. In addition, the legal profession holds attorneys to very strict parameters when it comes to publicly expressing their value. Chad recognized these two situations and successfully built his LinkedIn and overall digital strategy accordingly.

Chad's Tips

1. Figure out who you want to connect with. Have a plan and find ways to make a deeper connection with those people. I would rather have 10 strong connections than one hundred that know nothing about him.

2. People like to be recognized. Make deeper connections by sending congratulations, thank you e-mails, endorsing people, and writing recommendations.

3. Participate in key groups. I post helpful information in my groups. I don't worry about competition. If the info is helpful to me in my practice, I share it with my groups.

4. Build your brand and keep it consistent. You know who you are and what you want to be; if you want to be an expert in an area, everything you do should be built around that topic.

Chad helps individuals and businesses plan for success by using legal and business principles. To discuss strategy with Chad, please go to www.LeadGen2020.com/chadvanhorn or call him at 954-765-3166.

39

It's Not about Selling— You Have to Educate and Provide Great Information

Daszkal Bolton's Success

Stories abound online about people that claim to know all the insights to beat Google's algorithms. Perhaps some people do, but most of those claims are meaningless on multiple levels, and this next success story proves that. If you want to become one of the most highly recommended certified public accounting and financial consulting firms serving South Florida, you don't do it by trying to beat an algorithm. You do it through sharing information that benefits your target audience.

Your First Deal May Not Come so Quickly but if You Don't Start, It Will Never Occur

The firm we are describing is Daszkal Bolton and, it is headed by Michael Daszkal. Through his leadership, the firm has grown from a two-person firm to over 115 professionals. They've grown by consistently providing value to those they interact with, and they've adapted that philosophy to LinkedIn as well. Daszkal Bolton uses LinkedIn to differentiate themselves, show their value, educate their team, learn about their clients, and to stay very engaged with their clients.

They've made LinkedIn training mandatory for everyone in their firm. During that training, they teach their roadmap for LinkedIn success. Part of this training focuses on traditional elements, such as helping their team highlight expertise through effective use of their profiles. However, one very interesting thing they also do is help the team create the mindset for being proactive on LinkedIn and seek out people to interact with.

Clearly, this is a hurdle for many people, but the more you do it, the easier it becomes.

Armed with this training, you see many of the firm's employees sharing information within their specific areas of expertise. They post industry information, remind people about key deadlines, and share other valuable insights they've learned.

Love of the Boston Red Sox Helped Generate a New Client

While this is not an absolute, due to the stringent rules that need to be followed in accounting, tax, and auditing, sometimes it is difficult to distinguish one accounting firm from the next. Thus, differentiation is critical, and the best firms tend to have firm partners that are very astute at demonstrating this trait. One of the biggest successes that Daszkal Bolton has generated through LinkedIn came as a direct result of one of their partners using LinkedIn to help create his differentiation. This particular partner turned his love of the Boston Red Sox into a proposal, which then converted into a client.

Here's what happened. There was a particular bid that the firm was pursuing. As an astute business developer, the partner went on to LinkedIn to learn as much as he could about his prospect. He found people they knew in common, saw that this decision-maker was a big Red Sox fan (just like he was), and also found additional points of commonality.

In general, what is the best way to "break the ice" and build the relationship? Find common points of interest, and with LinkedIn, this is very easy to do. The prospect appreciated the "homework" the partner had put into learning about him and his business. The firm gained a new client, and the new client gained a trusted business advisor.

Michael's Tips

1. Constantly update your profile. Add skills, charity work, groups, associations, etc.

2. Don't be afraid to share a link or story. Avoid sharing fluff. It is all about sharing value and keeping your name in front of the people you need to be in front of.

3. Focus on quality over quantity.

4. It doesn't matter how late you are to the game; you can learn fast and still become effective.

Daszkal Bolton is an award-winning accounting firm serving clients with strategic solutions for all their accounting and business advisory needs. For their value proposition, visit www.LeadGen2020.com/daszkalbolton.

Rule

40

Podcasting + LinkedIn Generates Conversions

Kris Gilbertson's Success

What does podcasting have to do with success on LinkedIn? Actually, a lot if your success on LinkedIn is generated by your ability to tap into and deeply engage with an audience that is becoming harder and harder to find. Kris Gilbertson, author of *Podcasting 2.0: How to Generate Free Leads, Traffic, and Sales by Partnering with iTunes* (www.lifestyleacademy.com), shared with us how she is using LinkedIn with podcasting to generate conversions for her business.

Engagement on a Deeper Level

Podcasts reach a unique audience. Like many of us, this audience is comprised of people with business issues that need to be solved. The unique thing about this audience is that they are actively trying to seek out and engage with experts that can potentially solve these problems—on the go. They are also willing to take action when they find a solution. Thus, podcasting creates a very unique opportunity to generate quality interaction which engages on a deeper, more personal level.

Imagine podcasting and LinkedIn are like brother and sister, minus the bickering. Think of podcasting as the Chatty Cathy sister, like a conduit. It is a channel for conveying your personality and bringing your written content to life full of color and tone, simply by the power of your voice. It enables you to drive traffic wherever you choose.

Now, think of LinkedIn as the brother, like the connector, that captures all of that traffic from your podcast. When you direct your listeners and audience to your LinkedIn profile, it solidifies your connection and allows you to connect one to one now with a highly targeted lead for your business.

LinkedIn Is the "Door Opener"

Kris shared her strategy of using the podcast to create engagement, and using LinkedIn to seal the deal for a real solid connection. People tune in to listen to her during her weekly podcasts with key experts in the areas of business, marketing, and mindset. She shares her LinkedIn vanity link for people to come and learn more about her. Kris gets frequent invitations from this method, but for those that might be a little timid about connecting, she finds a way to engage them too. Each day, Kris reviews who has viewed her profile, and then she sends a custom note inviting these people to connect with her.

Typically, Kris spends about 30 minutes a day on LinkedIn. The accessibility to her and the credibility LinkedIn offers her have been the "door opener" for new business. Once someone from her target audience connects with her on LinkedIn, she integrates an "old technology" to generate business. She likes to engage with new connections over the phone. It gives her a better opportunity to build a stronger one-to-one relationship, and it enables her to get above the online noise too. Over the past year, Kris has generated multiple clients as a direct result of them connecting with her on LinkedIn and, most recently, even landed a new joint venture opportunity that will be kicking off right around the time this book is being released.

Kris' Tips

1. Have your profile where it is simple to understand. Make sure there is an effective use of keywords.

2. Keep your summary short, but communicate your value. To borrow from Susan Harrow, focus on using sound bites for your target audience.

3. Integrate a call to action within your profile so you can offer your target audience a sample of the value you can drive to them.

Kris coaches business owners to create a lifestyle business by launching world-class podcasts that generates free traffic, leads, and sales. Learn more at www.LeadGen2020.com/kris.

41

11 Clients from LinkedIn before Having a Website

Mary Agnes Antonopoulos' Success

When we talk about a conversion (i.e., success) on LinkedIn, it doesn't necessarily mean that the sentence ends with the statement "...and I sold thousands of dollars." Success can be from using LinkedIn as a conduit to connect with potential business partners or collaborate or to learn more about people you are prospecting with. However, the ultimate end point is usually consistent, and that is to leverage this platform toward a revenue generating activity either directly or indirectly.

Throw Away Your Marketing Budget

One of the most "direct" LinkedIn stories we've had the pleasure of learning about comes from Mary Agnes Antonopoulos (www.llnkedin.com/in/maryagnes/). Interestingly, success for Mary Agnes is not specifically direct revenue. She won't overlook it, but she defines success on LinkedIn as being engaged so deeply that someone in your target audience reaches out to you.

She was very open talking with us, sharing some very interesting insights and not looking for anything in return. Listening to her tell her story was very entertaining. She had us laughing with her at some of her marketing stories.

Let us try to set the backdrop for this particular story. She was an early adopter for LinkedIn. It is the early days of LinkedIn and social media. MySpace is dominating the social space. It seems that social media is just for teenagers and 20-somethings. In terms of business social media, no one has the definitive path to follow or even knows if this will work for people older than 30. However, that is not stopping people from experimenting. Enter Mary Agnes.

She initially started as an open networker on LinkedIn and was a frequent user of the old LinkedIn Answers function. For those who don't recall this feature, it functioned as a question-and-answer platform and was a tool that created strong engagement. From these two strategies, she built a significant group of connections and relationships. By October of her first year, she decided to create an offer for her contacts. She was laughing as she shared that this offer was sent out on the Friday **before** Columbus Day weekend—probably not the best time to send a marketing offer. Mary Agnes sent out a message to her "list" with the headline, "Throw away your marketing budget, hire her for 1,100 dollars for six weeks to do your social media campaign." By Monday morning, without a business website (which was still 18 months away), she had 11 new clients.

What Next?

The inspiring thing here was this was Mary Agnes' first foray into selling marketing. Seven years later, she still has one of the original clients! However, her client list since then has become very impressive. If you go to her website (www.rockawaywriter.com), she shares that she has worked with over one thousand other entrepreneurs, authors, speakers, and corporations including, Jack Canfield and Panera Bread.

For seven years, she has been teaching a free online class. She doesn't try to upsell people. As she put it, she tries to stay pure and she is going to continue with that. As she continues to evolve her business, she shared she is working on a new offering. This will be a paid one, teaching one topic per month plus two coaching sessions for a nominal fee.

Mary Agnes' Tips

1. In everything you do, tag it with your name, title, and phone number. Take the risk to be intimate the way that you can on LinkedIn.

2. Don't ask for anything; just be there as a great resource.

3. Put video on your profile. It's easy and right now, and it also sets you apart. Video is our best ambassador after face-to-face.

42 Generating Your Conversions

We've shared 41 rules that have highlighted LinkedIn's ability to support the lead generation process. Perhaps Harvey Mackay said it best through the title of his classic book on networking, *Dig Your Well Before You Are Thirsty.*[10] Hopefully through the creation of your "roadmap for results," you will be successfully digging the proverbial "well" for yourself and your business.

As we've shared, our methodology for "digging your well" starts with "strategy," followed by "awareness generation," which then requires "engagement." Successfully working these elements together puts you on the path to your desired "conversion." Interestingly, a conversion is a relative term. It doesn't mean the same thing to each person.

Examples of a successful conversion from your use of LinkedIn could be:

- An outright sale, new client, etc.

- More reach (i.e., attracting more traffic and more inquiries)

- Increased communication with your prospects, highlighting your credibility

- Many more things

---

[10] Harvey Mackay, *Dig Your Well Before You're Thirsty: The Only Networking Book You'll Ever Need* (New York: Currency/Doubleday, 1997).

Thus, we felt the best way to highlight conversions to you was by showing you different examples of how others have created success on LinkedIn.

Now, we are going to "break" the rules and turn it back over to you. It's your turn to generate your rules and define your conversions. We look forward to hearing about how they've helped generate your results. Please drop us a note.

If these 42 rules aren't enough for you, we have more available for free. We call these our "supplemental rules" and they can be downloaded for free at www.LeadGen2020.com/morerules.

#1 Fast Facts

With millions of people on LinkedIn, for those who are trivia inclined or statistical buffs, LinkedIn is rich in information. We thought it might be fun to look at some of the initial fast facts from the first edition and see how they compare now during the second edition.

Fast Facts

- **Founded:** Late 2002

- **Launched:** May 2003

- **Located:** Mountain View, California

- **URL:** http://linkedin.com/

- LinkedIn went public on May 19, 2011, at 83 dollars per share, which was an 84 percent rise from its initial price of 45 dollars.[11]

- Value: as of June 12, 2013, the stock price was at $167.12, creating a valuation of $18.44 billion dollars. Since the company was private when the first edition came out, there wasn't a lot of publicly accessible information. We did know that they had raised over one hundred million dollars and the company had mentioned they were profitable.

---

[11] Associated Press, "LinkedIn hits $83 at opening," Philly.com, May 19, 2011, http://articles.philly.com/2011-05-19/news/29560681_1_linkedin-profiles-zynga-groupon.

- Cofounder Reid Hoffman[12] is the largest shareholder in the company. Other large shareholders include Sequoia Capital, Greylock Partners, and Bressemer Venture Partners, all of who were part of that initial one-hundred-million-dollar investment.

- Employees: there were over three hundred when the first edition came out. Now there are just under four thousand (as of March 2013).[13] Using rounded numbers, that projects to a value of about 4.5 million dollars per employee (18 billion dollars per four thousand people).

- At the time of the first edition, LinkedIn's average user was 41 years old. According to Pingdom, the average age is now 44.2.[14] In addition, that report indicates that 79 percent of LinkedIn users are over 35 years of age.[15]

- As of November 2008, there were over 30 million registered users. As of June 2013, there were over 225 million.[16] LinkedIn was adding 30 people per minute in November 2008. As of this writing, the number is about 120 per minute.

- It took 494 days for LinkedIn to reach one million users.[17] Now, they do this about every five days.

- Groups: looking for one to fit your target audience? Well, there are over one million groups on LinkedIn to choose from.

- Company pages: there are over two million as of this writing. Expect that to increase dramatically in the near future.

- 53 percent of business-to-business marketers have acquired a customer through LinkedIn, compared to 22 percent for business-to-consumer.[18]

- 39 percent of LinkedIn users have paid premium accounts.[19]

---

[12] Leena Rao, "LinkedIn's Largest Shareholders And How Much They Own," *TechCrunch*, January 27, 2011, http://techcrunch.com/2011/01/27/linkedin-shareholders/.

[13] "About LinkedIn," *LinkedIn*.

[14] Pingdom, "Report: Social network demographics in 2012," *Royal Pingdom* (blog), August 21, 2012, http://royal.pingdom.com/2012/08/21/report-social-network-demographics-in-2012/.

[15] Ibid.

[16] "About LinkedIn," *LinkedIn*.

[17] "LinkedIn : Funny and Interesting Facts," *Daksh Branding*, accessed August 2013, http://www.dakshbranding.com/index.php/linkedin-funny-and-interesting-facts/.

[18] Sara Davidson, "Where Do Marketers Get Customers? [Data]," *Hubspot* (blog), May 23, 2013 (9:00 a.m.), http://blog.hubspot.com/where-do-marketers-get-customers.

[19] "THE LINKEDIN PROFILE," *Lab42*, accessed April 2013, http://lab42.com/infographics/the-linkedin-profile.

B Beware of Addictive Behavior

I may be a LinkedIn addict, but I also have the best-connected network of anyone I know.

Disclaimer: this is meant to be a light-hearted review of people spending too much time on LinkedIn. It is not intended to address any addictions.

If the first thing you do in the morning when you hop out of bed is to log into LinkedIn, then you may be a LinkedIn Addict (LA). If left untreated, it can lead to sleep deprivation, marital problems, and possibly generate no revenue.

10 Warning Signs:

If you think you are a suffering LA, take the quiz below. Just answer "true" or "false" to each statement.

1. You find yourself accessing LinkedIn first thing in the morning and last thing before you go to bed at night in addition to sneaking peeks during the day.

2. You become angry or agitated when your access to LinkedIn is slow or prevents you from connecting.

3. Given the choice of reading a book or spending time alone, you choose LinkedIn.

4. You check the number of "connections" you have more than once a day.

5. Your Google searches consist of finding new material related to LinkedIn. You talk in terms of your friends as first-, second-, or third-level connections.

7. It makes perfect sense to you to use something called "answers" to ask questions.

8. At family and/or business gatherings, you're hitting people up to see if they are on LinkedIn and interested in connecting with you.

9. You would rather spend time on LinkedIn versus spending time with your spouse/family/partner/significant other (well, sometimes this might be a good thing).

10. The hair on the back of your neck stands up when someone mentions that Facebook is a social networking site for business.

If you answered "true" to one or more of these questions, you may be LinkedIn Addicted.

Now that we have identified characteristics of a LinkedIn Addict, let's try to put a face with a name. The first person that comes to mind would be the Doc from the movie *Back to the Future*,[20] all crazy-eyed and white-haired, yelling to Marty about the DeLorean and the time continuum.

On the other side of the spectrum, perhaps, we may envision a young Doogie Howser who may have progressed from an online diary (early version of social communication) to immersing himself into the cutting edge of social media. After all, as a teenage doctor, he sure had an original story to share.

It has often been said that social media addicts do not want to miss anything; they are glued to the services they use 24/7 as they feel they must have their finger on the pulse and be involved in everything and all conversations. It's almost like the old days with radio call-in contests. We all sat by the phones waiting to dial and be "the hundred and first caller." No, we couldn't dial too soon, but we had to dial quickly, and to manage this dichotomy, we needed to keep our finger on the rotary dialer (which, for you young people, was what we used before voice activation).

We have populated this book with more information, more tips, and more techniques for leveraging LinkedIn. So while we appreciate you reading our rules, please don't blame us if you become a LinkedIn Addict!

---

[20] *Back to the Future*, directed by Robert Zemeckis (1985; Universal City, CA: Universal Studios Home Entertainment, 2009), DVD.

C 42 Things You Can Do with LinkedIn

Early in the book, we asked you how you were looking to utilize LinkedIn. To help you answer that, we have provided a variety of perspectives from executives to small businesses to job seekers to functional things you can do. So, without further ado, here are 42 things you can do with LinkedIn:

1. Answer the question of why you are on LinkedIn

2. Update and expand your profile

3. Better yet, do an extreme makeover on your profile!

4. Create your "three-second elevator pitch"

5. Customize your LinkedIn URL

6. Endorse someone you know

7. Respond to someone who has endorsed you

8. Ask for recommendations

9. Like a post

10. Comment on someone's post

11. Ask for an introduction from one of your direct connections to someone they are directly connected to

12. Educate people on how and why you want to be contacted

13. Become adept at using the search function

14. Join and participate in a couple of relevant groups

15. Organize a group based around an area of interest to you

16. Continue to grow your connections and build a quality network

17. Send a non-default invite (e.g., write a note in the invitation)

18. Post an article of value in your activity stream

Functional Uses

19. Relationship-build with your target audience

20. Demonstrate your expertise through the sharing of information (no selling)

21. Gather business intelligence on your competitors

22. Career management

23. Job search and, conversely, talent acquisition

24. Use LinkedIn for market research

25. Keeping in touch

26. Learn more about your prospects, partners, and vendors

27. Nurture your leads

28. Integrate LinkedIn with your other digital marketing

Three Ways for IT Professionals to Use LinkedIn with Their Internal Customers

29. Connect with and build relationships within your company

30. Communicate what you are working to your users

31. Generate recommendations from your users—builds internal credibility

Three Ways Executives Can Use LinkedIn

32. Job search (just like everyone else)

33. Research and land board positions

34. Conversely, they can attract key employees, partners, and suppliers

Three Ways Small Businesses Can Leverage the Power of Communication

35. Build a company profile to engage more deeply with your target audience

36. Notify your contacts of significant news, prospects, closings, sales, opportunities, etc.

37. Stay current on what your business partners, vendors, former colleagues, and potential new recruits are up to in their professional lives

Three Ways for Job Seekers to Leverage LinkedIn

38. Check out LinkedIn jobs

39. Use LinkedIn to find relevant headhunters to talk to

40. Use LinkedIn to expand the network of people you already know and keep them abreast of your search

And in Closing

41. Play by the rules—don't abuse, don't invent, don't circumvent

42. Lastly, regardless of the preceding 41 things, make time for your spouse or significant other. We won't go into what can happen if you don't!

About the Authors

Chris Muccio is an award-winning entrepreneur who draws upon insightful experiences from his successful career in corporate America to guide business leaders on the most effective strategies to uncover profit and growth opportunities that result in rapid and sustainable improvements within their business. His insight on social networking is highly sought after.

Peggy Murrah is the owner of a highly successful web design and virtual assistance business, providing her clients with resources to succeed in the online world of business. Through her ongoing networking, she created strong business relationships with entrepreneurs across diverse industries, and facilitated many mutually beneficial connections among them.

42 Rules Program

A lot of people would like to write a book, but only a few actually do. Finding a publisher and distributing and marketing the book are challenges that prevent even the most ambitious authors from getting started.

If you want to be a successful author, we'll provide you the tools to help make it happen. Start today by completing a book proposal at our website http://42rules.com/write/.

For more information, e-mail info@superstarpress.com or call 408-257-3000.

Other Happy About Books

42 Rules of Social Media for Small Business

This book is the modern survival guide to effective social media communications and the answer to the question, "What do I do with social media?"

Paperback: $19.95
eBook: $14.95

42 Rules for B2B Social Media Marketing

Social media is changing the way people think about marketing. It's much more than pushing out the same content through new channels. The biggest shift is that communications is now bi-directional; you can (and must) listen to your customers rather than just talking to (at) them.

Paperback: $19.95
eBook: $14.95

Purchase these books at Happy About
http://happyabout.info/
or at other online and physical bookstores.

A Message from Super Star Press

Thank you for your purchase of this 42 Rules Series book. It is available online at:
http://happyabout.com/42rules/24hr-success-linkedin.php or at other online and physical bookstores. To learn more about contributing to books in the 42 Rules series, check out http://superstarpress.com.

Please contact us for quantity discounts at sales@superstarpress.com.

If you want to be informed by e-mail of upcoming books, please e-mail bookupdate@superstarpress.com.

CPSIA information can be obtained at www.ICGtesting.com
Printed in the USA
LVOW10s1049031013

355259LV00003B/190/P

9 781607 731009